I0107763

The End of Days

The Shocking Truth About The Times In Which We Live

SEAN EDWARDS

Edwards Publishing House

The End of Days:

The Shocking Truth About The Times In Which We Live

By Sean Edwards

Copyright © 2016 by Sean Edwards

All rights reserved. Written permission must be secured from publisher to use or reproduce any part of this book, except for brief quotations in critical reviews or articles.

Unless otherwise noted, all Bible quotations are taken from the New King James Version, Thomas Nelson, 1984.

Cover Design by Juan Lopez Design

Contact Sean Edwards at: Sean@EndOfDaysBook.com

www.EndOfDaysBook.com

Published by Edwards Publishing House.

ISBN-10: 0985771534
ISBN-13: 978-0-9857715-3-9

Table of Contents

Preface

Some people might wonder why I updated this book. There are several answers to that question.

First, I believe I have become a better writer since I originally published this book. After recently re-reading the book, I realized that I repeated myself often and used clunky, complicated language. I knew that I could do better. But that wasn't a big enough reason to update the book on its own, though it did nag at me.

Secondly, from the outset I wanted to include visual aids for some sections of the book. But the work involved just to write the book was somewhat overwhelming, and these visuals got pushed to the side.

Thirdly, and most importantly, I discovered that a handful of source material I referenced were not accurate. This was by far the biggest reason for the update. As I state in the introduction, I studied history in college. And one the biggest lessons you learn as a historian is to never take someone's word for source material. You must track down original sources yourself to verify that: a) they exist, and b) they are taken in context.

When I originally wrote *The End of Days*, I did a lot of searching through primary sources. I had questions, and I wanted answers. So, much of the book was built on solid historical analysis.

In the flurry of getting the book written, I also cut a few corners. It is embarrasing, but I did it. In certain sections (like the discussion on Matthew 24), I referenced other historians' writings and research without corroborating all of it myself. This is a major "no-no" in scholastics. But, I trusted these authors and assumed they did the leg work to support their arguments.

That was a mistake.

I knew better, and my conscious finally got the better of me. So I went back to corroborate the passages. I was shocked to discover that many of the references did not exist. I searched for several quotes from early church fathers, and I could not them. There were a lot of blogs (and other books) that quoted them as I had (with half-hearted citations), but there were no real sources for them.

This, obviously, put me into a scramble. Where my conclusions wrong? I didn't know, but they were definitely in question.

So I searched through more primary documents to find out what early church fathers *did* say. And I found a lot of new, stronger information.

Fortunately, my conclusions were not undermined.

Which means that at the end of the day, the main point of the book didn't change. But how we got there in a few places did.

I realized that in order to have historical integrity I had to update my book with the new references. I also new that I had to apologize for violating my own rules and publishing something that was historically inaccurate.

Therefore, I am sorry. I sincerely apologize for this lapse in judgment.

But I can assure you that his updated version is accurate in its references. I followed my own code and can say with all integrity that, to the best of my ability, this book is properly supported by primary sources.

And since I was updating the book anyway, I decided to clean it up as well. I clarified the clunky passages, and removed the duplicate content. I also created some basic diagrams to help explain certain points.

With that, I believe this update is a stronger, more concise, and more accurate version of *The End of Days*, and I am proud to present it to you.

I hope it challenges and inspires you to look at the world in an entirely new way.

Thank you for reading.

Sincerely,

Sean Edwards
Spokane, WA 2016

Introduction

Taking an honest look at our beliefs about the end times can be educational. And for many, it can also be unpleasant. This was certainly true for me. Abandoning the Antichrist and the tribulation was a journey that took me years. But I found that I had to do it in order to be scripturally sound, and I hope to illustrate why in this book.

Challenging the modern day view of the end times can seem like heresy to many. We accept the Antichrist, great tribulation, and rapture as canonized truth right along with the virgin birth and resurrection. But I assure you I am not a heretic. I believe in the virgin birth, that Jesus is the son of God, and in the infallibility of scripture. I believe in the miraculous ministry of Jesus Christ. His death and resurrection. And I believe in our commission to continue His work on the earth.

But I don't believe in the end of the world. How can that be?

When I entered college, I was a futurist, meaning I believed that the Bible predicted the end of the world in our future. Possibly even in my lifetime. When I left college, I was a preterist, meaning I believed that there wouldn't be an end of the world (at least not like the one we so often envision). It was quite a transition. And it wasn't an easy one. I fought it hard.

We have an odd fascination with the end of the world, myself included. I was engrossed by what appeared to be a clear correlation between scripture and modern events. It made me feel important because God had chosen me to live in a time when biblical prophecy was being fulfilled.

At the same time, as a student of history, I also grew an appreciation for accurate historical arguments. I learned how to identify a good or poor historical argument when I saw it. Let me illustrate.

At one point early in my education, I wrote a research paper defending the historicity of the Exodus. Mind you, the school I was attending was liberal and secular. I was not in Bible College. So defending anything "Christian" was dangerous. I was nervous through the whole process of writing it.

I wondered, "Will the professor challenge my faith and grade me down for being a Christian?" When I got my paper, I received a low grade with some powerfully critical comments written on it. But this was a rough draft, and the professor recommended that I meet with him to improve my final draft. This meeting made me nervous to say the least.

When I sat down at his desk, he leaned towards me, looked me square in the eye, and said, "I want you to know that I don't have a problem with what you said. But rather with how you said it." I was immediately at ease. He went on to explain how the manner in which I used supporting materials would not stand up to scholastic scrutiny. I needed to handle my research and my supporting documents better. He then taught me how to properly interpret primary sources (ancient documents), and other sources to construct a strong historical argument.

By the end of my education, I graduated with a double major in two eras in history. This same professor nominated me to graduate with honors because he thought I better understood the fundamentals of studying history than most of my peers. I do not say this to boast, but to illustrate how my education affected my walk with the Lord.

Through this process I learned foundational study skills that strengthened my understanding of God. It also taught me how to smell a bad historical argument from a mile away.

When I began to study eschatology, I was able to apply these same skills to the end times. I was excited to support my beliefs with my bourgeoning historical skills. But I discovered something rather unsettling.

Instead of strengthening my understanding of futurism (which believes that the "end times" lie in our future), my historical assessment called it into question. I found that futurist arguments were riddled with errors. I got rather upset. Some of my core beliefs were challenged, and I didn't like it.

Furthermore, the preterist position (which believes that the "end times" occurred in the 1st century A.D.) had the backing of strong historical and contextual arguments.

For instance, futurism made almost no attempt to understand how first century Jews would have interpreted Matthew 24. And it made no attempt to understand the Jewish idea of the "end of the age," which dramatically reshapes how we understand this portion of scripture.

As I studied, I found that preterists used historical evidence to support their view. They went to great lengths to put passages into context.

And though futurist arguments did the same, I found them weak and full of holes.

Furthermore, I found that futurism didn't take into account the historical parallels between the Book of Revelation and the destruction of Jerusalem.

As I read more and more, I became so upset that I threw my book against the wall. I didn't want to give up my Antichrist. I didn't want to give up my Armageddon. I felt as though someone was trying to steal a sense of significance I received from living in the last days. So I fought it for a long time.

But after years in eschatological limbo, I could no longer ignore the evidence. I accepted preterism.

I don't know what it is about the end of the world, but we have an odious obsession with it. Once a preterist, I started to ask myself: "Why was I so invested in the end of the world? Why did I want Jesus to come back immediately and condemn over four billion people to

Introduction

hell?" I still don't know, but I think it is a question we should ask ourselves. What condition of the heart makes us passionately defend the death of billions? If someone comes to us saying, "I have discovered that we can interpret scripture in a way that doesn't doom billions to a horrible death," why do we react violently rather than study to see if it is true?

When I discuss the end times with people, I get an array of responses. Some respond with skepticism. Some with joy. And others the way I did at first. They respond with anger, as they vehemently defend their Antichrist. And I understand it. I was the same way.

I am not asking you to give up your eschatology in this book. I'm just asking you to set it down for a moment. You can always pick it back up if you decide I'm wrong. I just want you to listen to what I have to say, because I believe it has the power to change your life.

I want to show you that God can be just without destroying the planet. I also want to illustrate how misunderstanding the end times can rob us from our great call in world history.

Part 1

PREPARING FOR THE END

In Steven Covey's book *The 7 Habits of Highly Effective People*, he tells a story that illustrates the importance of putting "first things first." You may have heard it.

The illustration goes like this: A professor stands in front of a group of people, pulls out a pitcher and places several large rocks in it until he couldn't fit any more. He then asked the students, "Is the pitcher full?" Everyone responded by saying, "yes."

Then the professor pulled out a container of gravel, and poured it into the container. He asked again, "Is the pitcher full?" More cautiously, some people said, "Yes."

Then he pulled out a container of sand, and poured it into the pitcher of rocks and gravel. He asked the students, "What about now?" This time the students said, "No." They had wisened up.

The professor said, "Correct." He then pulled out a container of water and poured it into the pitcher until it was full.

He then went on to explain the importance of "putting the big rocks in first." Because if you don't, you'll never get them in at all.

When it comes eschatology and Christians, this is an apt metaphor. Many Christians have lots of opinions about the End Times. But most of us have not taken the time to "put the big rocks in first." Meaning, we haven't been taught the fundamentals of proper bible study and interpretation.

We've made assumptions about God, the world, and our mission in it that aren't necessarily true. This first part of the book is about putting th big rocks in first. We can't jump straight into the Book of Revelation or Daniel without going over some basics. That would be like filling the pitcher with water before everything else. Our preconceptions about scripture and the End Times will stop any new information from entering our minds.

Therefore, in these first few chapters, we will cover the "big rocks." Things like whether the world is getter better or worse. The wrath of God. The identity of the antichrist. And the role of the Messiah in ancient Jewish tradition.

It may not sound as exciting as going straight to Revelation, but it will yield great fruit. Our understanding and appreciation of scripture will be transformed, along with the world around us.

Chapter 1

THE END OF DAYS

"For unto us a Child is born,
 Unto us a Son is given;
 And the government will be upon His shoulder…
 Of the increase of His government and peace
 There will be no end" – Isaiah 9:6-7

The world appears to be in a state of constant turmoil and deterioration. Earthquakes, hurricanes, and wars all seem to prove that the world is moving towards a cataclysmic end. News outlets bombard us with disasters, murders, and rapes. Peace in the Middle East seems more impossible than ever. The number of countries with nuclear weapons has grown. And the threat of a global economic meltdown seems ever more likely.

Should these events surprise the Church? These events appear to fulfill prophetic scriptures about the end of the world. For many, current events prove that we live in the last days. These people are certain that the Antichrist is right around the corner. They also believe that God will soon rapture us away. Passages in Revelation, Daniel, and other biblical books appear to describe these times. But is this true? Does scripture tell us that the end of the world is upon us?

Apocalyptic teachings on the end of the world have exploded in the last two hundred years. Many Christians expect to see the demise of civilization. Thousands of sermons, books, and teachings tell us that the Bible predicts this demise.

But what if it isn't true? What if there is another way to look at scripture that paints a different picture? One that also holds to traditional Christian ideas?

Most people refer to this view of the end times as "futurism." We call it futurism because it states that all the apocalyptic scriptures refer to events in our future. Futurism permeates our culture through movies, books, and TV shows. We have a fascination with the end of the world.

Yet many bible-believing scholars are not futurists.[1] And futurism has not been the dominant view of the end times for most of church history. The modern form of futurism, also known as "Dispensationalism," is only two hundred years old.[2] Our concepts like the tribulation,

1. Marvin Pate and others, *Four Views on the Book of Revelation* (Grand Rapids, MI: Zondervan, 1998), 17-18.

2. Clarence B. Bass, *Backgrounds to Dispensationalism* (Eugene, OR: Wipf and Stock Publishers, 2005), 64.

Antichrist, and rapture did not exist for most of Church history. Mainstream christian scholarship understood that the apocalyptic passages referred to the destruction of Jerusalem in A.D. 70.

For someone raised with a futurist worldview, this seems inconceivable. How could the end of the world have occurred two thousand years ago? The purpose of this book is to answer that question.

But for now, let us examine the significance of our end times perspective. Our view of the end times affects every aspect of our lives. It impacts the way we see God. It affects the way we see ourselves. It defines our purpose. Since our view of the end times influences so much of our lives, we need to be willing to make sure we are right.

No one polishes brass on a sinking ship. If we believe that the world will end in fiery judgment, we will make no effort to improve it. This is why many Christians are not worried about the planet and the environment. Since the world is going to burn anyway, it doesn't matter what we do to it. What if we're wrong? What if we're supposed to be stewarding the land, making it better?

In the 1970s, in the Jesus People movement, Christians dropped out of college at a staggering rate. They felt that school was a waste of time because the world was about to end. They wanted to spend their last days evangelizing the world to save as many souls as possible.

They had a great heart – but they were wrong. The world didn't end. The result was that non-believers completed their education and took professional jobs.

Most of which many Christians were not qualified to fill. The church abdicated its position of influence because it believed "the end was nigh."

Where would we be today if they hadn't dropped out of college? What would our movie industry be like? What would our courts look like? How would the business world function? We will never know because well-intentioned Christians had a wrong view of the end times.

The course of human history can be changed by what we believe about the end of the world. This means that we must be certain we are right. We can't afford to be wrong.

Eschatology, or the study of the end times, is a fascinating subject. There are as many ways to interpret scripture as there are stars in the sky. But most interpretations fall into four eschatological categories: Futurism, preterism, idealism, and progressive dispensationalism.

Futurism holds to traditional apocalyptic views. It states that all the apocalyptic passages refer to events in our future.

Preterism believes the apocalyptic passages refer to events in our past. Primarily, the destruction of Jerusalem.

Idealism understands Revelation to be a metaphorical image that comforts Christians in distress. It does not believe that the book of Revelation depicts literal events. Rather these images communicate that Jesus is still King in all situations.

Progressive Dispensationalism is stuck between futurism and preterism. It holds that "end times" passages have many fulfillments. It can accept both preterist and futurist arguments.

In this book we are going to look at preterism and futurism. We will challenge the dominant understanding of the "end of the world" in the Church. We will see that the enemy has deceived the Church into abdicating the future to evil. When we apply proper biblical and historical study tools to scripture, we will see that the world will not "end." There won't be an Antichrist or a Great Tribulation. We will see that the Church has missed her assignment.

God called her to spread the gospel and redeem the planet, not to announce its end.

A Doctrine of Demons

There is strong scriptural and historical evidence to show that futurism is flawed. Not only that, but it enables evil to prevail upon the earth.

Futurism misrepresents God as an angry Father. Yet scripture says He is love (1 Jn. 4:16). Futurism portrays the world as an evil place in need of judgment, but Jesus said He did not come to judge the world, but to save it (Jn. 3:17). Futurism anticipates evil to expand in the world, when scripture says that to the expansion of God's kingdom and His peace there will be no end (Is. 9:6-7). Futurism breeds anxiety and fear, when scripture says that God did not give us a spirit of fear (2 Tim. 1:7). Futurism believes Satan still has power, yet Jesus disempowered him two thousand years ago (Col. 2:15).

Finally, futurism presents an inaccurate description of objective reality. It states that the world is getting worse, but it isn't. By most metrics, the world is getting better. People are living longer, healthier, and wealthier lives than ever before (we will look at this in more depth in the next chapter).

And futurism has blinded millions from stepping into their God-given destinies.

To prove this, we will go through most of the scriptures that deal with the end times and offer an alternative interpretation. We will see that there is a strong argument for the preterist understanding of the end times. We will see that there won't be an Antichrist or a tribulation in our future. We will discuss things like:

- The Antichrist
- The Great Tribulation
- The Rapture
- Matthew 24
- The Prophesies of Daniel
- The Book of Revelation

We will discuss their misinterpretation and how to look at them in a new way. It is the purpose of this book to show that the Bible does not predict Armageddon. But instead it anticipates an improving world until it is completely redeemed.

Titus Flavius Josephus

We will be using Titus Flavius Josephus as one of our primary sources. Josephus is important because he was an eyewitness to the Roman conquest of Jerusalem in the first century. Secular historians have used his writings for centuries as reliable historical documents. Though, like any other historical documents, we need to take some of his comments with a grain of salt.

He was a Jew by birth and lived from A.D. 37 to A.D. 100. He fought against Rome as a Jewish general at the beginning of the First Jewish-Roman War. But Rome captured him at Jotapata. The Romans then drafted him to be an intermediary for them and the Jews.

The Wars of the Jews (known as "*Wars*" for short) is a detailed eyewitness account of the First Jewish-Roman War (A.D. 66 – A.D. 70).

Josephus was not a Christian. But his writings appear to describe events predicted in the Book of Daniel, Revelation, and Matthew 24. Because of his unique perspective, Josephus will be a prominent person in this book. [3]

This Changes Everything

The ideas held in this book have the potential to transform

---

3. Flavius Josephus, *The Works of Josephus: Complete and Unabridged,* trans. William Whiston (Peabody, MA: Hendrickson Publishers, Inc., 1987), ix.

your life, your church's life, and the course of history. When we understand that God is not coming to destroy the planet, but rather to redeem it, it changes our entire outlook on life.

There is an amazing saga unfolding around us: the complete redemption of human history.

Ultimately, it is the aim of this book to redefine the term "eschatology." Gordon Fee, in his work *Paul, the Spirit, and the People of God*, argues that Christians should be an eschatological people. Meaning that Christians, through the Spirit, should bring the future (eternity) into the here and now. When people see Spirit-empowered Christians, they should see what eternity will look like.[4] Eschatology, then, should not be a study of the end of the world. But rather it should be the study of the beginning of a new one. Eschatology is the key to understanding who we are today and what we're supposed to be doing. Eschatology is not the study of the end times. It is the study of our times.

---

4. Gordon Fee, *Paul, the Spirit, and the People of God* (Peabody, MA: 1996) 49-64, 124, 177.

Chapter 2

THE FALLEN WORLD

It is important to begin our study by laying some ground-work. First, we must look at the idea that the world is getting worse.

This is a major tenant of futurism. It anticipates an ailing world as we approach the end.

And most people believe that the world is spiraling towards collapse.

But it isn't. Almost every major metric indicates the opposite. It isn't even open for debate. To believe that the world is getting worse, in the face of these statistics, requires that we reject reality.

Over the last two hundred years humanity has seen astounding progress.

As a case study, let's look at world hunger trends. These figures come from the Food and Agriculture Organization of the United Nations:

- In 1970, the WHO considered more than 958 million people "chronically hungry."

- In 2010, there were fewer hungry individuals, but still a staggering 925 million.

- Yet, in 1970 the world population was only 3.7 billion.

- Whereas in 2010 it reached 6.8 billion.

- When you look at the ratio of hungry people to the relative global population, you see something astonishing.

- In 1970, 25.8% of the world was hungry.

- Whereas in 2010, only 13.6% were hungry.

- *That's a 47% decrease in 40 years.*

Over the last forty years, we have cut the relative number of hungry people in the world in half. We still have a long way to go to end hunger, but this shows dramatic improvement across the board. In short, we are taking ground, not losing it.

Almost every other metric shows the same trend. There are some down blips every once and a while, but the main trend is up.

In his book *The Improving State of the World*, Indur Goklany clearly illustrates this point. He uses statistics from government agencies and non-profits from all over the world. The evidence is clear. Human existence is getting better, not worse. Here are a few more examples:

Hunger. Goklany reaffirms what we've already seen. We are producing unparalleled amounts of food every year. This is due to breakthroughs in farming techniques and falling equipment prices.

In 1967, the average person worldwide consumed 2,254 calories a day. In 2002 that number had grown to 2,804 calories a day.[5] He goes on to break those numbers down into different countries around the world. For instance, the average Chinese citizens' daily food intake has gone up 80% since 1967. The average Indian's caloric intake has increased by 50%. Even sub-Saharan Africa saw a modest increase of 7%.[6] In summary, Goklany says, "Although the world's population has never been larger, the average person has never been better fed."[7]

Not only are people eating more food, but they can afford more of it. Once you take inflation into consideration, the price of food has dropped by 75%.[8] After crunching all the numbers, he states: "If a country's average income had stayed constant at a dollar a day (in 2000 international dollars), a level that is sometimes

---

5. Indur Goklany, *The Improving State of the World: Why We're Living Longer, Healthier, More Comfortable Lives On A Cleaner Planet* (Washington, D.C.: Cato Institute, 2007), 22.

6. Goklany, 23.

7. Goklany, 21.

8. Goklany, 25.

considered to be approximately at 'absolute poverty,' then prevalence of malnutrition in its population would have dropped from 79.5% to 58.6%."[9] Translated into English, people can buy more food with less money.

Infant Mortality. Just as we have seen with hunger, infant mortality rates are dropping all over the world. Before industrialization, one out of every five children died before the age of one. That translates to over 200 infant deaths per 1000 births. Worldwide, by 2003, that number had dropped to 57. That is almost a 72% reduction. In the United States, between 1900 and 2000, that number fell from 190 to just 6.6 – *a 96.5% reduction*. In China, between 1950 and 2003, infant mortality rates dropped from 195 to 30 per 1,000 births. India's rate dropped from 190 to 63.[10] Sub-Saharan Africa saw a drop from 177 to 101.[11] We still have a long way to go, but this paints a clear picture – infant mortality rates are dropping worldwide. Which means people around the world have greater access to medicine and food than ever before in history.

Life Expectancy. People are living longer than ever before, as well. For most of human history life expectancy has averaged between 20-30 years. Things didn't change much until 1900, when worldwide life expectancy hit 31. By 2003 life expectancy had climbed to a staggering 66.8.

---

9. Goklany, 26.

10. Goklany, 27.

11. Goklany, 28.

For wealthier countries like the United States that number reached 77.6. Developing countries saw an increase to 63.4. Sub-Saharan Africa saw a drop-off to 45 in the 1980s, due to HIV, but fortunately that trend is reversing.[12]

Prosperity. For the first one thousand years after Christ, most people lived on one dollar a day (in 2000 international dollars). By the 1800s, that had grown to $650 a year (or $2 a day). By 2001 that had surged to $6,000 a year – that's a 923% increase. Wealthier countries have done better, but every country has seen an explosive growth in wealth. And since the price of food has dropped, people can buy more food.

Literacy. From 1970 to the early 2000s, global literacy rates grew from 54% to 82%.[13]

Political Freedom. Today, we consider 44.1% of the world "free," meaning they do not live under an oppressive government. 18.6% are partially free. That means only 37.3% of the world lives under oppressive governments. What other era in human history can say that?[14]

The Good Ol' Days

What about the "good ol' days"? Weren't things better back then? Well, lets look at the "good ol' days."

---

12. Goklany, 36.

13. Goklany, 46.

14. Goklany, 47-48.

For women, was life better two hundred years ago or today? Less than one hundred years ago, women couldn't vote in the United States. Over fifty years ago, it was acceptable to ignore domestic abuse.

What about modern medicine? Things that would have killed us one hundred years ago are just nuisances now.

Furthermore, the modern world has abolished the institution of slavery. No other era of history can say that.

If we believe the world is getting worse, then in what other era would we have rather lived? When would life have been better than it is today?

We idealize the past, and in doing so, we forget that plague, war, famine, and death were constants for most of human history. Though there are things about the world we may not like, we cannot deny that we live in the best epoch of human history.

Fact or Fiction?

Some Christians don't think statistics have a bearing on the matter. To them, the improvement of the natural world could be a spiritual deception. So they disregard these facts in an attempt to maintain scriptural integrity.

Yet, this creates serious problems. If we cannot trust what we see and feel, how can we know anything at all? Some might say, "I trust scripture and the Word of God more than I trust statistics or facts of the world." But even then, you must trust your senses to be relaying real and true information.

You must read (your sense of sight) scripture or you must hear (sense of hearing) a preacher. Even to trust the Word of God, we must decide that our natural senses can relay true information to our minds. If we can't trust what our senses are telling us, then we can't trust scripture... what if our eyes are deceived? We can't trust preaching... what if our ears are deceiving us? At some point, we must make a leap of faith to trust our senses. Otherwise, we can know nothing at all. And this is all statistics are. Observations made of the natural world. We can debate how that information was collected, or how it is presented. But at the end of the day, we must trust what we observe.

This line of thinking also reveals a disconnect between the natural world and the spiritual world that did not exist two thousand years ago. We want to break the world in two... there is spirit and there is matter. And we like to think that they can (and do) exist independent of each other. This means that things can appear to be getting better in the natural world, but the spirit realm could be getting worse. Therefore, statistics have no bearing on the reality of the world.

This is Greek in nature and not Jewish, nor biblical. It was the Greeks who decided that spirit was inherently good and matter inherently evil. It was the Greeks who first decided that we could not trust our senses. Not the Bible.

In the Christian world today, part of this disconnect comes from a misinterpretation of Paul in 2 Corinthians. He says: "While we do not look at the things which are seen, but at the things which are not seen. For the things which are seen are temporary, but the things which are not seen are eternal." (2 Cor. 4:18). This can lead many to discount the natural world as a deception.

But Paul did not say that the physical world was a deception. He said it was temporal, meaning it can change. Whereas the Kingdom is constant. The physical world is still real and true. But the Kingdom will stand throughout time.

Also, Hebrews states, "By faith we understand that the worlds were framed by the word of God, so that the things which are seen were not made of things which are visible." (Heb. 11:3). This verse implies that the invisible world (the spirit realm) shapes the visible world (the physical world). It says that the spirit realm forms the foundation and inner structure of the physical world.

Therefore, the natural world is a picture of the spirit realm. The spirit realm can't be getting worse while the physical world gets better. That is not how things work. They are integrally linked. This means that if the natural world is getting better, then good things are happening in the spirit realm as well.

Thus, statistics about the material world can–and do– tell us the true state of the world. If things are getting better... things are getting better. It is that simple.

Things Are Not As They Appear

We cannot look at the facts and continue to believe the world is getting worse. To do so would require us to deny reality. But if the world is getting better... why does it seem like its getting worse?

Our personal experience may seem to contradict these statistics. So how do we reconcile that with global trends?

One answer rests in the proliferation of information. The Internet, computers, and iPhones have given us instant access to catastrophes. News from all over the world now bombards us all the time.

One hundred years ago, it would have taken a long time for these stories to cross the country and the globe. And only a select few made the journey.

But today, we can hear about a car bombing in Bagdad, a murder in Atlanta, and a serial rapist in Paris, all in thirty seconds. Yet none of these stories would have been available to us in previous generations.

This constant access to news can make it appear that more bad things are happening. But in reality we are just seeing more of what has already been happening.

Another reason things may seem worse has to do with news outlets. News agencies are like any other business. They need to make money to survive. They do this by airing commercials for other businesses. But businesses won't buy those spots unless the station can prove that it has a large audience. So the news stations must compete with each other to hold onto viewers.

In recent years they have discovered that people are more likely to watch bad news over good news. Research has found that the brain reacts faster to negative stories, and it also remembers them better. Other studies have shown that 7 out of 10 news stories must be negative in order to keep an audience. That means that only 30% of their content can be good or neutral reporting. Otherwise people won't watch or listen to their channel. This means that in order to sell advertising, they have to fill their airtime with negative news stories. Thus, no matter what outlet you watch, it won't be objective.

Some are quick to blame the media for problems in our culture. But it isn't their fault. It is ours. They are catering to their audience and offering the only product we will buy. If we want to blame someone for our negative media, we need to look in the mirror.

Evil Isn't Growing – Principalities Are Falling

Another reason things appear to be getting worse has to do with "revealing evil." When dark things come into the light, it can make it look as though the world is getting worse. Let's take domestic violence as an example.

For thousands of years, societies have looked the other way when men abused women and children. In many places it was even encouraged. Over the last century, that has changed. People's eyes have opened to the injustice of domestic violence and there is an active campaign to purge it from society.

But now that we have brought this abuse into the light, it appears as though domestic violence is on the rise. When in fact it is on the decline. People recognize its evil, and the modern world has rejected it. This is progress.

When this happens, a principality is falling to the name of Jesus. A demonic power sat over domestic violence for centuries going unchecked. It had deceived the nations into thinking it was a good way to manage a household. Now, Christ has bound this principality and it is falling.

You can say the same thing about rape in the Middle East. Or female circumcision in African countries. Or human-trafficking. These horrible things have been around for thousands of years. Oftentimes endorsed by their cultures. But not today. More and more people all over the world have woken up to their barbarity. And they are working to purge them from the earth.

Unfortunately, much of the Church is not leading the charge in these battles because it expects these things to happen. Instead of doing something about it, Christians shake their heads and say, "It's just the signs of the times." This is tragic because Christ gave us the authority to end these injustices, *and we aren't using it*.

The Church has been deceived into thinking the world is getting worse. Our eschatology is at the root. At some point, someone told us that the Bible said the world would get worse... and we believed them.

Yet, nothing could be further from the truth. The Bible actually anticipates a gradual improvement in the world. But we must re-examine the assumption that the world is getting worse. It has profound implications on our role in the world.

Chapter 3

PIERCING THE LIES OF THE ENEMY

One reason our eschatology has gone off course comes from our poor biblical interpretation skills. When we look at a passage in scripture, we need to use proper interpretive principles to determine its meaning. Otherwise, we can end up thinking a passage means the opposite of what the author intended.

Within much of the Church, there has been a reaction to "academic" approaches to scripture.

You can be academic and attuned to the Spirit at the same time. The idea that one is either a "person of the Word" or "a person of the Spirit" is an oxymoron. You can't be one or the other. If you want to be a person of the Spirit, the Word must ground you. And if you want to understand the Word, then the Spirit must lead you.

God gave us intelligence and the ability to recognize reason. Let's not cast it off, displaying our willful abdication of thought as a point of pride.

Yet, holding too close to a set of interpretative tools can inhibit your spiritual growth as well. Our principles can keep us from hearing God. They can lock us in spiritual infancy and fill us with useless knowledge. Proper interpretive tools should keep us grounded in scripture, and also lead us into an encounter with the Author. Anything less, and we are depriving ourselves of our greatest Treasure.

The number one principle in interpreting scripture is this: Our interpretation of a passage must be consistent with how the original audience would have understood it.

When an author records a story, or writes a letter, they have a purpose in writing it. There is an audience to whom they are writing. And they have a message they are trying to convey. If we want to understand a passage, we must discover to whom the author was writing and what he was trying to say.

Interpreting a portion of scripture without doing this puts us in great danger. We can come to a conclusion the author never intended.

Here's an example. Let's say you are traveling abroad on mission work. At one point, you decide to write a letter to your family, telling them that you will visit them soon. Now let's say your family forwards that letter to some of their close friends. Those friends would know that you were writing to your family and not to them. They would also understand that you were not coming to visit them. It would be absurd for them to open your letter and say, "Hey, John is coming to visit us soon!" If they did, it would mean they ignored your original message and the intended audience.

But this is what many well-meaning Christians do to scripture. They assume that a passage was written to them. They do not understand that they are thousands of years removed from the actual intended audience.

For the most part, this is not our fault. Christians aren't taught to properly interpret scripture. But fortunately it isn't that hard.

The first step is by identifying a passage's cultural, historical, and scriptural contexts.

We start this process by taking a close look at the historical context of a passage. The historical context is the world in which the author wrote the passage. In what time period did the author live? In what part of the world did they live? What language did they speak? How did they use different phrases and idioms? What clothes did they wear? How did they travel from place to place? What were their religious and spiritual beliefs? What was happening around them (wars, famines, etc...)?

If we don't ask these questions, we will arrive at wrong conclusions. This is especially dangerous with passages like Matthew 24.

Many Christians view Matthew 24 as a prediction of the end of the world in our future. But this passage is a conversation Jesus had with a real group of people during a specific point in history. If we don't attempt to understand what He was trying to say to those people, then we will miss His point (we will look at Matthew 24 in greater detail in a later chapter).

Not only must we look at the historical context of a passage, but we must also examine the scriptural context as well. This is where a passage lands within a story, history, or letter. Quite often verses immediately before and after a passage pertain to its meaning. For instance, Matthew 24 occurs right after Jesus announces the coming judgment of Jerusalem. This affects how we view Matthew 24. Without recognizing this we are ignoring a pivotal aspect of the narrative.

When biblical authors recorded these episodes, they were not writing to us. They were writing to a group of people thousands of years ago.

When Matthew sat down to write his account of Jesus' life, he had an intended audience in mind. It wasn't us. This must influence how we understand a passage.

This does not mean that scripture can't speak to us. Or that God doesn't speak to us personally through scripture. In fact, God uses scripture to talk to us all the time. God will also sometimes take a passage out of context to communicate with us (He has the right to do that–He wrote it). Yet, it is important that we know when He does this.

Before we build a theology on a verse or a passage God spoke to us, we need to make sure we understand the author's original intent. Otherwise we could take a word that God meant for our personal journey and build a corporate theology out of it. This could lead people into heresy. If God speaks to you and takes a passage out of context, find other scriptural support for what He said before you take it to other people. This does three things: 1) It strengthens our understanding of scripture. 2) It leads us into further revelation of the Word. 3) And it makes sure we aren't listening to an evil spirit masquerading as light.

Once we apply these principles to the apocalyptic passages, what we discover will shock us. In the next chapter will study the Antichrist as an example.

Chapter 4

THE ANTICHRIST

*(**Note:** when discussing the Antichrist as a person, the term will be capitalized. When discussing the antichrist as a concept or spirit, it will not.)*

For most Christians, the Antichrist plays a central role in our faith. He is the main antagonist in the end times struggle. He is the figure that leads the world into a revolt against God and His people. The end times without the Antichrist is like a Bible without Jesus. It just doesn't seem possible.

Yet, scripture never says any of these things about the "Antichrist." The term "Antichrist" is never mentioned in the Book of Revelation, the Book of Daniel, or the Gospels. Paul never uses it in any of his epistles. And in never shows up in any of the Old Testament.

In fact, the term "antichrist" is only found in two letters written by the apostle John. And those passages have nothing to do with the end of the world. Here is every biblical passage that contains the term "antichrist":

> "Little children, it is the last hour; and as you have heard that the **Antichrist is coming, even now many Antichrists have come**, by which we know that it is the last hour... Who is a liar but he who denies that Jesus is the Christ? **He is Antichrist who denies the Father and the Son.**"[15]

> "For many deceivers have gone out into the world who do not confess Jesus Christ as **coming in the flesh**. This is a deceiver and **an Antichrist**."[16]

> "Every spirit that confesses that Jesus Christ has come in the flesh is of God, and **every spirit that does not confess that Jesus Christ has come in the flesh** is not of God. And **this is the spirit of the Antichrist**, which you have heard was coming, and **is now already in the world**."[17]

These are the only passages in the bible in which you will find the antichrist. Before we analyze these passages, lets break down the word "antichrist." "Christ" means "anointed one" or "Messiah." So, "antichrist" means literally "anti-anointed one" or "anti-messiah."

---

15. 1 John 2:18, 22, emphasis added.

16. 2 John 7, emphasis added.

17. 1 John 4:2-3, emphasis added.

In the above passages, John describes the antichrist as a spirit, not a particular person, which can influence anyone. He claims that anyone who denies that Jesus came in the flesh is an antichrist. Furthermore, he goes on to say that "many antichrists have already entered the world," and that they were already among those to whom he was writing.

John was writing to a small Christian community two thousand years ago. Which means that there were many antichrists already in the world in the first century.

These passages do not discuss the end times. They are a warning against false teachers and apostles.

Two thousand years ago, the early church was battling a heresy known as Gnosticism. It threatened to undermine the foundations of the Church.

Gnostic teachers argued that "the Christ" was a spirit and did not have a physical body. This concept was attractive to Greco-Romans because it lined up with Platonism. Platonism taught that all matter was evil and that God could never touch it. In His ultimate perfection, He would destroy it upon contact. Thus Gnostics rejected the idea that Jesus was both fully God and fully man. God would never take on physical form, much less suffer death.

Many Gnostic Christians reconciled these ideas in an interesting way. They taught that the "Christ-spirit" (which was a lesser divine emanation, so it could touch matter) came upon the man Jesus and inspired him to teach. But upon his death, the Spirit left Jesus' body.

This ideology threatened the foundations of the Church. If Christ did not have a physical body, then He could not have died on the cross. If He did not die on the cross, then He could not have paid for our sins. If He did not pay for our sins, then we weren't saved. Salvation itself was undone by this teaching. And it was spreading throughout the Church like wildfire.

So, John refers to gnosticism as the "antichrist" spirit. He is saying that the spirit behind gnosticism stood against Christ.

John understood the antichrist to be a spirit that attempted to dismantle Christ's atonement.

The Last Hour

John goes on to say that they were living within the "last hour" (I Jn. 1:18). Many take this as evidence that we are living in the last hour. But, once again, we must remember that John wrote to a group of people two thousand years ago. He was warning his flock to watch out for teachers carrying a deadly deception. This warning can apply to us, in the sense that we should watch against heresy, but it has nothing to do with the end of the world.

We immediately assume that when John said "the last hour" he meant the last hour before the end of the world. But He didn't say that. He just said that they were in the last hour… with no more clarification. He could have been referring to the "last hour" of local persecutions. Or the "last hour" before the fall of Jerusalem. Or any number of other subjects. The point is that he never clarified the "last hour." The audience must have already known its meaning.

And John could not have been referring to the end of the world. He wrote these letters two thousand years ago to a specific church in Asia Minor... and the world hasn't ended. If he had been discussing the end of the world, it would have meant nothing to his audience. Why mention it? How did a warning about the end of the world thousands of years removed pertain to their struggle with a gnostic heresy?

The modern view of the Antichrist comes from a blend of several different figures found in scripture. Most notably the Book of Daniel, Matthew 24, and the Book of Revelation. Yet, as we will discuss, we can identify these figures as separate historical persons. Poor interpretive principles cause us to blend them together into a figure known as the Antichrist.

Scripture reveals that there is no "Antichrist." The antichrist spirit was the inspiration behind a deadly teaching in the early church. One that threatened the foundations of orthodox Christianity. It was not a person inspired by Satan to usher in the end of the world.

Chapter 5

THE RAPTURE

Next we need to examine the concept of the rapture. Contrary to popular belief, the modern idea of the rapture is only two hundred years old. Church theologians have argued for centuries about the exact nature of the rapture. But those debates did not include what we believe today.

The modern view of the rapture has Jesus rapturing the church right before, during, or after (depending on your particular eschatology) the Great Tribulation and the rise of the Antichrist. At some point, those Christians still alive will be taken off the planet. Then judgment will fall on the rest of the world.

But some may be shocked to learn that these ideas first appear in the writings of John Gill (1748) and Morgan Edwards (1788).[18] Most christians at the time considered

---

18. Harold Eberle and Martin Trench, *Victorious Eschatology: A Partial Preterist View, 2nd Edition* (Yakima, WA: Worldcast Publishing, 2009), 284.

these ideas bizarre. In 1830, the Plymouth Brethren were the first substantial group of Christians to accept this concept as real. The Brethren were a small group that held unorthodox ideas. Their peers rejected most of their theology and questioned their interpretation of scripture.

But in 1909, Scofield inserted the Brethren's ideas into his study bible and they spread around the world with great speed.[19] And they quickly became the mainstream view of most Christians. Modern futurists will admit that the idea of the rapture is new.[20]

Now, just because this idea is new does not mean it is wrong. But it should cause us to study it carefully before we accept it.

The Scriptural Root of the Rapture

Most Christians use I Thessalonians 4:13-17 to discuss the rapture. It says:

> "But I do not want you to be ignorant, brethren, concerning those who have fallen asleep, lest you sorrow as others who have no hope. For if we believe that Jesus died and rose again, even so God will bring with Him those who sleep in Jesus.

---

19. Bass, 150.

20. Harry Ironsides, who wrote about the Powerscourt Prophetic Conferences (strongly influenced by the Plymouth Brethren), stated, "It was in these meetings that the precious truth of the rapture of the Church was brought to light.", Bass, 41.

For this we say to you by the word of the Lord, that we who are alive and remain until the coming of the Lord will by no means precede those who are asleep. For the Lord Himself will descend from heaven with a shout, with the voice of an archangel, and with the trumpet of God. And the dead in Christ will rise first. **Then we who are alive and remain shall be caught up together with them in the clouds to meet the Lord in the air. And thus we shall always be with the Lord.** Therefore comfort one another with these words." (Emphasis added)

Verse 17 is the main verse used to defend the rapture. But when we understand the context of the passage, and study the underlying Greek, we will see that it is not.

First, Paul is attempting to comfort the church in Thessalonica (v. 18). They were worried that those who died before Jesus' return would not enjoy the same rewards as those who were still alive. This gives us context. This is the question he was answering. Thus, how we interpret this passage must make sense as an answer to that question.

Second, the Greek word translated as "caught up" is *harpazo*. The Latin version of the bible translated this as *rapio* (where we get "rapture"). *Harpazo* has several different meanings. It can mean to physically remove something (like Philip in Acts 8:39).[21] But it can also

---

21. Timothy Friberg, Barbara Friberg and Neva F. Miller, vol. 4, *Analytical Lexicon of the Greek New Testament*, Baker's Greek New Testament library, 75 (Grand Rapids, Mich.: Baker Books, 2000).

mean "an ecstatic vision or experience" in which one is "caught up" or "away" in the Spirit. [22] To determine what Paul meant, we need to look to see if he uses this word elsewhere. And he does.

In 2 Corinthians 12:2, Pauls says that he knew a man (most believe he was talking about himself) that had been "caught up" in the third heaven. He describes it as an "ecstatic" experience, not a literal one. This means that Paul has a precedent for using *harpazo* in a spiritual manner.

Because of this precedent, it is safe to assume that I Thessalonians 4:17 refers to an "ecstatic vision or experience," and not a physical event.

This passage also discusses the resurrection of the dead, which places the event at Jesus' final return. Not at some point before it. Paul states that the dead will rise and all the saints from history will "meet" Jesus "in the clouds." He places this event at the consummation of eternity.

Furthermore, the word Paul uses for "meet" (Gk, *apantesis*) means the Church will be part of Jesus' return. We will not leave the world for a time and then return. In ancient cultures people would "meet" dignitaries as they entered the city. The New American Commentary corroborates this usage in I Thessalonians 4:17:

> "In secular Greek the word [used here for "meet"] was a technical term for meeting a visiting dignitary. A delegation honored the visitor by going outside the city and

---

22. *Analytical Lexicon of the Greek New Testament*, 75.

meeting him and his entourage on the road. Together the entire party would then proceed back into the city with great pomp and fanfare."[23]

Paul is not talking about the church leaving the planet. He is saying that we, along with the resurrected dead, will welcome Him back to the Earth as the eternal King.

Furthermore, clouds symbolized the presence of God in the Old Testament. [24] Movement into the presence of God can be described as movement into "the clouds."[25] Thus, when Paul says that we will "meet" Him in the clouds, he means that we will be drawn into His presence.

Paul is not saying that the church will be raptured from the earth while Jesus dispenses judgment. Paul is discussing the first moments of eternity. The dead will rise and every Christian will be "caught up" in Jesus' presence through an ecstatic experience that signals His return. This passage in 1 Thessalonians 4:13-17 comforted the church in Thessalonica by telling them that all the saints, both dead and living, will be part of Jesus' glorious return.

---

23. D. Michael Martin, *1, 2 Thessalonians*, vol. 33, The New American Commentary (Nashville: Broadman & Holman Publishers, 1995), 153.

24. See Exodus 19:16; 24:15–18; Ezekial 1:4, 28; Isaiah 19:1; cf. Ps 97:2

25. D. Michael Martin, *1, 2 Thessalonians*, vol. 33, The New American Commentary (Nashville: Broadman & Holman Publishers, 1995), 153.

Chapter 6

THE WRATH OF GOD

"There is no fear in love. But perfect love drives
out fear, because fear has to do with punishment.
The one who fears is not made perfect in love."
– 1 John 4:18

As we continue to lay a new foundation about the end
times, we need to discuss the wrath of God. Most people's
eschatology involves a fiery view of God's judgment. For
them, Jesus will return at some point and judge the earth
for its sin. He will purge evil from the earth and establish
eternity. Many also believe natural disasters are a sign
of God's judgment.

This understanding of God's character is not based on
New Testament theology. It does not give an accurate
picture of the Father's heart. And it causes us to proclaim
judgments that did not originate in heaven. Passages
from the Old and New Testaments reveal that God is no

longer angry with us. Nor will He judge the world in a final moment of wrath. God's wrath and judgment are things of the past.

In fact, in order for Him to be just, He can no longer judge sin.

"Cheap" Grace

For God to be just, He must punish sin. Thus, God must judge the world for its sin. This "judgment view" of God is an Old Covenant idea. The defining act in the New Testament is the atonement of Jesus. His sacrifice on the cross paid the price for all sin.

This is basic Sunday School 101. Yet many fail to understand its implications. Or how it changed the nature of our relationship with God.

Paul said that Jesus "crucified sin in the flesh" (Rom. 8:4), meaning that Jesus killed sin. He executed it. Jesus also stated that He "came to fulfill the law" (Matt. 5:17), meaning that He met all the righteous demands of the law. His sacrifice is total and complete. He "made one sacrifice for sins forever."[26] No other sacrifice is necessary.

If Jesus died for all sin, what is left for Him to judge?

Many will object and say that within the same verse Jesus says, "He did not come to abolish the law." They will argue that God still has high standards for sin. And if we disregard that, we are living under "cheap grace."

26. Hebrews 10:12

They call it "cheap" because it doesn't cost us anything.

But, grace isn't grace if it costs you something. It is either freely given or it isn't grace at all. Otherwise, it is a wage–something you have to earn.

The Greek word Jesus used in Matthew 5:17 for "abolish" means to pull apart or dissolve into nothing. Jesus said that He did not come to dissolve the law into nothing. That would be unjust.

The word Jesus used for "fulfill" means to "completely fill up."

Think of the requirements of the law as a barrel. Jesus said He did not come to tear the barrel apart, but instead to fill it. Justice for every sin in the world created the barrel. But Jesus came and filled the barrel for us. There is no more room in the barrel. There are no more demands of justice.

The law hungered for justice, and it was always demanding that sin be punished. Jesus came and gave it what it wanted. Now it no longer demands justice.

For Jesus to make this clarification in Matthew 5, His teachings must have sounded a lot like "there is no more law." Or else why would He have had to clarify Himself? His message was so close to this that He needed people to understand that God was still just.

Furthermore, Paul makes a startling statement in I Corinthians about sin and judgment: "All things are lawful for me, but not all things are helpful; all things are lawful for me, but not all things edify."[27] Paul states that everything is now lawful. But not everything is good for him.

Paul was writing to a group of Christians who thought that God's grace nullified anything sinful they did. The shocking thing is that Paul says they were right. He says that God wouldn't judge them for anything they do. But why would they want to continue living in sin? Christ's sacrifice kept them righteous before God. But that kind of lifestyle wouldn't lead them into everything God had for them.

If Jesus paid the price for all sin, how can God still judge it in our lives? Either Jesus paid the price or He didn't. There is no middle ground.

If Jesus paid for all sin, and God still punished people for it, God would be judging the same sin twice. Once on the cross, and once today. This is not just. In fact, in the United States it is illegal to do this. It's called double jeopardy.

The Nature of Atonement

Some might argue that grace only extends to those who have accepted it. Thus, God still judges nonbelievers. This raises a good question: Does Christ's atonement pay the price for everyone's sins? Or does it only cover the sins of those who accept it?

Isaiah 53 tells us the Messiah would pay for everyone's

---

27. I Corinthians 10:23

sin: "All we like sheep have gone astray; We have turned, every one, to his own way; And the Lord has laid on Him *the iniquity of us all.*" Isaiah didn't say, "And the Lord has laid on Him the iniquity of those who follow Him."

Furthermore, John makes it clear that Jesus' paid for everyone's sin: "And He Himself [Jesus] is the propitiation for our sins, and not for ours only *but also for the whole world.*"[28] John made it very clear. Jesus' atonement covered the sins of everyone. Even those who are not following Him.

This does not mean that everyone will go to heaven. If people go to hell, it is not because God sends them there for judgment. It is because they choose to live eternity apart from God.

God cannot judge the world today for sin. If He did, He would be committing double jeopardy. He would be an unjust God. God did those things in the Old Testament, but Jesus changed everything. Now, in order for God to be just, He must extend grace to everyone.

Justice Without Punishment

Still not convinced? Lets look at some more passages. In the Gospel of John, Jesus states: "the Father judges no one, but has committed all judgment to the Son."[29] This

---

28. 1 John 2:2

29. John 5:22.

means that all judgment has been given to Jesus. Then, later in John, Jesus makes a radical statement:

> "I have come as a light into the world, that whoever believes in Me should not abide in darkness. And if anyone hears My words and does not believe, **I do not judge him; for I did not come to judge the world but to save the world**. He who rejects Me, and does not receive My words, has that which judges him— the word that I have spoken will judge him in the last day."[30]

Jesus states that He will not judge anyone, even if they reject Him. Earthquakes, tsunamis, and plagues are not His instruments of judgments anymore. We are in an epoch of grace.

Jesus does say that there will be judgment on the last day. But He doesn't say that He will judge people. He says His word will judge them. How can a word judge someone?

His teachings lead people out of darkness and into light. His teachings broke the bonds of the enemy. Choosing to reject that offer would keep you in bondage. The judgment Jesus describes is the choice to stay in bondage. They aren't being judged for their choice; their choice is their judgment. Jesus even describes it as such elsewhere:

> "For God did not send His Son into the world to condemn the world, but that the world through Him might be saved.

---

30. John 12:47-48, emphasis added.

He who believes in Him is not condemned; but he who does not believe **is condemned already**, because he has not believed in the name of the only begotten Son of God. **And this is the condemnation, that the light has come into the world, and men loved darkness rather than light, because their deeds were evil.**"[31]

Jesus states that belief in Him will free you from condemnation. But those who don't believe in Him will remain in condemnation. No new condemnation comes upon them. He will not judge them for their choice. Rather they already stand in condemnation.

He goes on to define this condemnation: "And this is the condemnation, that the light has come into the world, and men loved darkness rather than light, because their deeds were evil." He states that their condemnation is that they chose to live in darkness and reject the Light. They chose to live in corruption. They chose to drink water infested with parasites. They chose to experience pain, suffering, and loss. They chose sin, sickness, and death over the abundant life Jesus offered them.

Jesus does not offer grace in one hand and judgment in the other. He shows us the path to clean waters, green pastures, and eternal life. He says that if people refuse His offer, they will stay in their hellish pit.

This is such a radical view on the grace of God that the disciples didn't understand it at first. At one point, Jesus and the disciples were on their way to Jerusalem.

---

31. John 3:17-19, emphasis added.

They wanted to pass through a Samaritan village, but the village did not allow them to enter. James and John were so offended that they asked Jesus if He wanted them to call fire down on the village. Jesus' response should speak to us when we are tempted to do the same:

> "And when His disciples James and John saw this, they said, "Lord, do You want us to command fire to come down from heaven and consume them, just as Elijah did?" But He turned **and rebuked them**, and said, **"You do not know what manner of spirit you are of. For the Son of Man did not come to destroy men's lives but to save them."** And they went to another village."[32]

Jesus said the disciples were out of alignment with the Spirit of God. Had they been in alignment with the Father's heart, they would not have asked to judge the village. Yet, the church today cast judgments against people and places all the time. If Jesus were standing next to us, do you think He would endorse our actions? Or would he rebuke us and tell us that we are not in alignment with the Father's heart?

The Old Testament Predicts Grace

When people look at the Old Testament and see God's wrath and judgment, they fail to interpret it through the

---

32. Luke 9:54-56, emphasis added.

lens of the New Covenant. They assume God is still angry. But that season is over. Jesus demonstrates that the Spirit of God does not inspire declarations of judgment.

Furthermore, God doesn't like judging people. Isaiah 54:7-10 tells us that judgment grieves His heart. He hated it so much that He found a way to never be angry with His children again:

> "For a mere moment I have forsaken you,
>   But with great mercies I will gather you.
>   With a little wrath I hid My face from you for a
>   moment;
>   But with everlasting kindness I will have mercy on
>   you,'
>   Says the Lord, your Redeemer.
> "For this is like the waters of Noah to Me;
>   For as I have sworn
>   That the waters of Noah would no longer cover the
>   earth,
>   **So have I sworn**
>   **That I would not be angry with you, nor rebuke**
>   **you.**
>   **For the mountains shall depart**
>   **And the hills be removed,**
>   **But My kindness shall not depart from you,**
>   **Nor shall My covenant of peace be removed,'**
>   Says the Lord, who has mercy on you."[33]

God equates anger at His people to the pain He felt when He flooded the earth. He hated the flood so much that He promised never to do it again. This is one of the few

---

33. Isaiah 54:7-10, emphasis added.

passages in the Bible where God says that He "regretted" His decision.

Isaiah tells us that God feels the same way when He is merely angry with His children. He hated it so much that He thought of a way to make sure He would never have to be angry with us again. That was Jesus' death and resurrection.

When Jesus died on the cross, He satisfied the wrath of God. In verses 9 and 10, God states that He will not be angry with us. Nor will He rebuke us again. And even if the mountains fall away and the hills crumble, He will never be angry with us again. That leaves little room for God's wrath and judgment today.

Some may believe this verse is referring to eternity, and that it doesn't apply to today. But just a few verses later in this same passage (verse 15), God says that people will assemble against His people. But they will fail to harm them. This puts this passage on this side of eternity.

No Fear In Love

Our view of God and the end times does not line up with God's character and what He said He would do. Jesus said that the devil came to steal, kill, and destroy. But Jesus came that we should have abundant life (John 10:10). Which does our eschatology sound more like? Abundant life—or death and destruction?

For many, anger and fear surround the end times. People need to repent, they say, lest God judge them. But it is "the kindness of God that leads men to repentance" (Rom. 2:4).

God does not motivate by fear, but by love. 2 Timothy 1:7 states that "God has not given us a spirit of fear, but of power and of love and of a sound mind." John says that God is love (1 John 4:8). If anyone claims that fear is a part of love, John states otherwise:

> "There is **no fear in love**; but perfect love casts out fear, because fear has to do with punishment. But he who fears has not been made perfect in love."[34]

John says that God's love casts out all fear. He says that we do not have to fear God anymore, for His Son paid the price and received all the Father's wrath. John says that fear stems from punishment. John is saying that those who fear have not been perfected in God's love. They don't understand that God isn't going to punish them.

Fear is a terrible motivator, and God knows it. When you're scared you are not at your best. You don't listen to reason. You just want to run or hide. Your brain releases adrenaline and you are thrown into "fight or flight" mode. On the other hand, you are the most creative and productive when you are at peace. Fear does not make you a better lover. Fear is rooted in preserving your life; once you have done that, fear shuts off and your motivation ceases. How can that produce love? It can't. Fear is the motivator of slave masters, not fathers.

---

34. 1 John 4:18, emphasis added.

Fear is the mortal enemy of love. God never wanted to motivate us with fear. If we look at Psalm 32:8, we see that this has always been His desire:

> "I will instruct you and teach you in the way you should go; **I will guide you with My eye**. Do not be like the horse or like the mule, Which have no understanding, **Which must be harnessed with bit and bridle**, Else they will not come near you."[35]

God does not want to guide you with fear and punishment (the bit and bridal). But with intimacy and love (His eye).

When fear motivates you, you "lack understanding" and need the use of a bit and bridle. But when love motivates you, you are far more creative, loving, and productive.

When love motivates you, you obey out of your care for the other person's heart, not fear of punishment. The reason you choose not to sin isn't because you're afraid of judgment, but because you are in love with God. This is what God desires with us.

In summary, fear and God's wrath are entrenched in our understanding of the end times. Futurism tries to use fear to motivate people into the Kingdom. And fear is a direct byproduct of Futuristic eschatology. Yet, John says God is love and that there is no fear in love. Furthermore, if Jesus paid the final price for all sin, then there is no room for punishment. It would be illegal for

---

35. Psalm 32:8, emphasis added.

God to punish us again. Because of what Jesus did, we are unpunishable.

The Discipline of the Lord

What about discipline of the Lord? God does discipline us, but our culture has confused discipline and punishment. In our culture, discipline means a spanking. But that is punishment, not discipline. Discipline comes from the same root as "disciple," which means, "to learn." Discipline is learning, training, and preparation. It is not punishment.

Discipline can be grueling and hard. Training for a marathon requires great discipline, and is often painful and brutal. Yet it isn't punishment.

Performing surgery is another example. It requires great discipline (long hours of study, reading, and practice). But it doesn't require punishment. The discipline of the Lord is as if He is saying, "I know you're tired, but if you want to achieve all that I have for you, you need to run one more lap." It's when we've given everything we have to our relationships and God says: "I know this hurts and that you want to quit, but if you want what I have for you, then you need to push through this. Trust me, I will guide you."

There are several passages in the New Testament that are used to defend the idea that God punishes. But many of our translations have been influenced by our false concept of God's anger. For instance, the NIV renders Hebrews 12:5-6 as such:

> "My son, do not make light of the Lord's discipline, and
> do not lose heart when he rebukes you, because the Lord
> disciplines those he loves, and he **punishes** everyone he
> accepts as a son."

This passage quotes Proverbs 3:11-12. But there are two
versions of the Old Testament available to us. There is the
Hebrew Old testament (known as the Masoretic text) and
there's the Greek Old Testament (called the Septuagint).

The Hebrew and Greek versions of the Old Testament
render Proverbs 3:11-12 different. The author of Hebrews
quotes from the Septuagint (the Greek version). The
Hebrew version says:

> "My son, do not despise the Lord's discipline and do not
> resent his rebuke, because the Lord disciplines those he
> loves, as a father the son he delights in."[36]

So, why are these verses different? Jewish scholars translated the Old Testament into Greek in the 3rd century B.C.,
because Greek had become the common language at that
time. They wanted scripture to be accessible to people
whom only spoke Greek. And just like any language, the
meanings of words change over time.

At some point in our past, the English word "discipline"
meant "to learn." But it has come to mean "to punish".
It is possible that the Greek translation of the Old Testament used words that were accurate when it was first

---

36. Prov. 3:11-12, emphasis added.

translated, but became askew centuries later when the author of Hebrews quoted from it. Jews may have even understood the original meaning of the word, but those of us centuries later can't make the distinction.

The important thing to take away from this is that the Hebrew version (the original language) states that God disciplines those He loves. It does not say that He punishes those He loves.

Another common defense of God's punishment is Revelation 3:19. Jesus states: "As many as I love, I chasten and rebuke." But the word for "chasten" means to convict or expose, which is different from "chastise." Then, the word for "rebuke" means to teach, like you would teach children at school. Revelation says that Jesus shows you when you're walking down the wrong path. What loving father wouldn't do that? But that isn't punishment. It's correction.

The discipline of the Lord can be hard and difficult, but it's not a punishment. It's training and preparation. Jesus died so that God didn't have to punish you. He wants to guide you into all that He has for you, and sometimes that road is difficult.

The Fear of the Lord

People also stumble with the "fear of the Lord." If "there is no fear in love," then why does the Bible say that "the fear of the Lord is the beginning of all wisdom?"

We hear most about the fear of the Lord in the Book

THE END OF DAYS

of Proverbs. Solomon states that the fear of the Lord is the beginning of wisdom and source of life.

When you look at the Hebrew word for "fear," it has a couple of different meanings. It can mean "fear" in the traditional sense. But it can also mean: "revere, venerate, i.e., show profound respect for one, that borders on fear of the object…"[37] This kind of fear is different than the fear associated with most end-times predictions.

It occurs in those moments when His greatness comes out of the clouds and you realize just how big He is. It happens when you want to fall down on your face in front of Him. Not because you're afraid, but because you're suddenly aware of His "bigness."

This is the fear of the Lord. This indescribable reverence for God that borders on fear, yet is not actually fear. These are humbling moments, but they are never scary moments. In fact, once you understand how much God loves you, they produce great intimacy. God doesn't want us cowering in fear of Him. That era is over. A new era has begun.

Ananias and Sapphira

The story of Ananias and Sapphira raises another question about punishment. Lets examine this passage:

---

37. James Swanson, *Dictionary of Biblical Languages With Semantic Domains: Hebrew (Old Testament)*, electronic ed., DBLH 3707, #2 (Oak Harbor: Logos Research Systems, Inc., 1997).

"But a certain man named Ananias, with Sapphira his wife, sold a possession. And he kept back part of the proceeds, his wife also being aware of it, and brought a certain part and laid it at the apostles' feet. But Peter said, 'Ananias, why has Satan filled your heart to lie to the Holy Spirit and keep back part of the price of the land for yourself? While it remained, was it not your own? And after it was sold, was it not in your own control? Why have you conceived this thing in your heart? You have not lied to men but to God.'

Then Ananias, hearing these words, fell down and breathed his last [...]

"Now it was about three hours later when his wife came in, not knowing what had happened. And Peter answered her, 'Tell me whether you sold the land for so much?'

"She said, 'Yes, for so much.'

"Then Peter said to her, 'How is it that you have agreed together to test the Spirit of the Lord? Look, the feet of those who have buried your husband are at the door, and they will carry you out.' **Then immediately she fell down at his feet and breathed her last.**"[38]

This verse can't mean what it appears to mean on face value: that God kills liars. If that were true, then we would all be dead. So, there has to be another explanation.

It is possible that this passage speaks more towards

---

38. Acts 5:1-10, emphasis added.

Peter's apostolic authority rather than God's judgment.

We have this notion that God has all the power and we have none. Part of that statement is true: God does have all power, but He has given that power to us. Jesus said that He was sending the disciples out just as the Father sent Him.[39] He said they would have the same power and authority He had. In fact, He says that they will do even greater things than Him.[40] He even states that we can bind things in heaven. In the Great Commission, He stated that He had all authority in Heaven and on earth. Then He sent out the disciples in that authority.[41] Jesus states that everything the Father possesses has been given to Him, which He then gives to us.[42] Finally, He says that we even have the ability to forgive people's sin, which is something only God could do until the New Covenant.[43]

The New Testament authors had a dramatically different understanding of the authority we have. The Bible appears to describe apostles as individuals with incredible authority on earth.

Furthermore, Peter was set aside as the preeminent apostle.[44]

---

39. John 20:21

40. John 14:12

41. Matthew 28:18

42. John 16:15

43. John 20:23

44. Matthew 16:18

Finally, Proverbs says "Death and Life are in the power of the tongue." [45] There is power in what we say. When we declare things over ourselves and others, they affect us. When God created the universe, He "spoke" everything into existence. We are His children and have His DNA. Our words can create or dismantle realities.

Thus, it could be that Peter declared judgment over Ananias and Sapphira, and it killed them. Jesus said we could forgive or withhold forgiveness. We also know that Peter was walking in great authority because people were healed just by touching his shadow. Could it be that this wasn't an act of divine judgment? But rather a display of apostolic power? Many will find this concept difficult to swallow, but it deserves consideration.

---

45. Proverbs 18:21

Chapter 7

THE NEW ISRAEL

Many Christians link the restoration of Israel to the end of days. They believe that God's plan for global redemption (or judgment) centers around Israel, and that the last days will begin as He fulfills unfulfilled promises to Israel. The reconstituted nation of Israel in modern times has contributed to this expectation.

Some Christians state that if you want to know what time it is on God's clock, look at Israel. Because of this, there is a strong emphasis placed on Israel in the church. Yet this dichotomy between the church and Israel is a modern belief.

Once again, the Plymouth Brethren in the mid 1800's (who introduced the modern rapture theory) created this division. Later theologians built upon it to produce what we now call Dispensationalism. There is a lot more to dispensationalism, but this split between the church and Israel is a key component of it.

The Brethren first developed this distinction from their strict interpretation of scripture. They required a literal fulfillment of every prophetic passage. For them, they could not "spiritualize" anything. Thus, they concluded that all the promises for Israel in the Old Testament are still reserved for them. They were not transferred to the Church. Instead, Israel will receive them at some time in the future.

Dispensationalists hold that Jesus brought two kingdoms when He ministered. Jesus offered a physical Kingdom to the Jews, which they rejected. Then Jesus offered a spiritual Kingdom to the gentiles. But ultimately God will finish His work with Israel.[46]

This brings us to the defining characteristic of Dispensationalism. God's entire redemptive plan centers around His covenant with Israel. The Church becomes more of an "interruption" of God's plan rather than the fulfillment of it.[47]

For most of church history, there has been no split like this. Theologians believed Jesus offered a spiritual Kingdom to the Jews, but they rejected it. They were expecting a physical kingdom like that of David. When Jesus didn't offer that, the Jews rejected Him. He then offered the Kingdom to the gentiles, who became the New Israel. And all the promises given to Israel were transferred to the Church.

---

46. Bass, 30.

47. Bass, 25.

Dispensationalists fiercely contest this idea. They call it "replacement theology." Yet Paul clearly states that the Church is the new Israel:

"Therefore remember that you, once Gentiles in the flesh—who are called Uncircumcision by what is called the Circumcision made in the flesh by hands—that at that time you were without Christ, being **aliens from the commonwealth of Israel and strangers from the covenants of promise**, having no hope and without God in the world. But now in Christ Jesus you who once were far off **have been brought near by the blood of Christ**.

"For He Himself is our peace, **who has made both one, and has broken down the middle wall of separation**, having abolished in His flesh the enmity, that is, the law of commandments contained in ordinances, **so as to create in Himself one new man from the two**, thus making peace, and **that He might reconcile them both to God in one body through the cross**, thereby putting to death the enmity. And He came and preached peace to you who were afar off and to those who were near. **For through Him we both have access by one Spirit to the Father**.

"Now, **therefore, you are no longer strangers and foreigners, but fellow citizens with the saints and members of the household of God**, having been built on the foundation of the apostles and prophets, Jesus Christ Himself being the chief cornerstone, **in whom the whole building**, being fitted together, **grows into a holy temple in the Lord**, in whom you also are being built together **for a dwelling place of God in the Spirit**." [48]

48. Ephesians 2:11-22, emphasis added.

Paul was a Pharisee. If there had been any separation between the Church and Israel, he would have mentioned it. But he didn't.

Rather, he states that God has "made both [Jew and Greek] one" and that "in Him [Jesus]" He created "one new man from the two." Paul says that Christ brought down the dividing wall between Jew and gentile. In its place He formed one new man.

We are now one in Christ. It is faith in Christ that makes us the "heir of Abraham's covenant" (Gal. 3:16). Not our ethnicity.

Paul says that the Father is building us (Jews and Greeks) together to form a "dwelling place of God." He says:

> "Therefore, there is no distinction between Jew and Greek, for the same Lord over all is rich to all who call upon Him. For 'whoever calls on the name of the LORD shall be saved.'"[49]

The only criteria for being part of the New Man is calling upon Jesus in faith.

Paul states that there is still a salvation for the Jews. But they must recognize Jesus as the Messiah to receive it. Paul says that the Jews were "broken off" because they did not believe Jesus was the Messiah.[50] Yet, if they

---

49. Romans 10:12-13

50. Romans 11:20

accept Christ, God will graft them back onto the tree.[51]

Some Christians use Romans 11 to claim that God is not done with His covenant with Israel. In it, Paul states:

> "I say then, has God cast away His people? Certainly not! For I also am an Israelite, of the seed of Abraham, of the tribe of Benjamin. God has not cast away His people whom He foreknew." (Rom. 11:1-2)

This verse seems to imply that God still has a plan for Israel. Paul goes on to say that there is a remnant within Israel that God has set aside for redemption. Some Christians think this means that God has a group of Jews today that He will exalt and redeem. But Paul says these Jews are the remnant because of the "election of grace." They are Jews who believed in Christ.

We know this remnant is Christian because Paul says that they achieved their election by grace (Rom. 11:6). He says that the remnant were not selected because of the law or the old covenant, but because they believed in Jesus.

When Paul says that God has not cast away His people, He means God has not eternally blocked Israel for salvation. There is still a road to redemption for them, just as there is for everyone. But that road does not come from their covenant. It comes through Jesus.

When God judged Israel with Babylon, He said that Israel's sin had become so severe that repentance could

---

51. Romans 11:23

not stop the coming judgment (see Jer. 11:11, 14). Paul is saying that this is not one of those times. God will gladly graft them back in… as soon as they accept Jesus.

Paul even states: "What then? Israel has not obtained what it seeks; but the elect have obtained it, and the rest were blinded." (Rom. 11:7). Paul says that Israel did not get what they wanted. They lost it and the Church got it. Paul says that God did not make them stumble so that they would completely fall. They stumbled, and that opened the Kingdom to the gentiles, but they can stand again. They were knocked down, but not out. To illustrate this, Paul uses a picture of a tree:

> "And if some of the branches were broken off, and you, being a wild olive tree, were grafted in among them, and with them became a partaker of the root and fatness of the olive tree, do not boast against the branches. But if you do boast, remember that you do not support the root, but the root supports you.

> "You will say then, "Branches were broken off that I might be grafted in." Well said. **Because of unbelief they were broken off,** and you stand by faith… **And they also, if they do not continue in unbelief, will be grafted in**, for God is able to graft them in again. For if you were cut out of the olive tree which is wild by nature, and were grafted contrary to nature into a cultivated olive tree, how much more will these, who are natural branches, be grafted into their own olive tree?" (Rom. 11:17-24).

Paul illustrates that the people of God are like a tree, supported by the root, Jesus. The Jews were "broken off" because of unbelief. They are no longer connected to the root and they are not the people of God. But, that does not mean their rejection is eternal. If they believe in Jesus, God will graft them back into the tree.

Paul states that in order to be part of the New Israel, you must believe in Jesus. Their covenant and ethnicity no longer makes them the people of God: "They are not all Israel who are of Israel, nor are they all children because they are the seed of Abraham."[52] To be a part of the true Israel, and to be a true seed of Abraham, you must have faith in Christ.

When Christ came, He changed everything. God wiped away the Old Covenant and built a new Israel in its place.

Jesus came and established the Kingdom of God. He brought about the end of the previous age. He established a new world order known as the Church. Because we accepted Christ, we are now the recipients of the Old Testament promises. Paul said that we were once "aliens... from the covenants of promise" but that we have "been brought near by the blood of Christ." Through Jesus, the Church inherited all the promises of God.

There is no longer a distinction between Greek or Jew, slave or master, or male or female in the Kingdom. Through faith in Christ, Paul tells us that we are one new

---

52. Romans 9:6-7

man, being built up together to be a holy resting place for the Spirit of God.

Praying for Israel is good. Loving Israel is great. And we should respect them for *at one time* being God's people. They have special gifts and blessings because of that past. But scripture makes it clear that God removed their place of preeminence in the world and gave it to the Church. This means that Israel shouldn't receive any more attention from us than any other people group. They do not hold a special place in God's redemptive agenda. The church is not an ellipses in God's plan. The church is God's plan. We are His people. And His plan for humanity flows through us.

Part 2

THE FULFILLMENT OF DANIEL

"But you, Daniel, shut up the words, and seal the book until the time of the end... and when the power of the holy people has been completely shattered, all these things shall be finished." – Daniel 12:4, 7

We will start our scriptural study of the end times with the Book of Daniel. Daniel plays a huge role in most people's eschatology. It contains many passages that have led to exciting and terrifying predictions about the end of the world.

Many Christians read Daniel and think it predicts events in our future. But the historical context of Daniel makes this unlikely.

In the 6th century B.C., God judged Israel for their lack of faith. He used Babylon to do it. After Babylon destroyed Jerusalem, they carried many of the Israelites back to Babylon. Daniel was among them.[53] The Bible records this as the "Babylonian Captivity." Most of the visions in Daniel pertain to the fate of the Jews, not Christians, or the end of the world.

We have to look at these passages in context. And we must ground them in history. Once we do this, we will see that they are about events that occurred in our distant past.

---

53. Daniel 1:1-4

Chapter 1

THE HISTORY OF DANIEL

To better understand the Book of Daniel, we need to examine the history surrounding Daniel's prophecies. This may seem tedious, and just a list of names and dates to many, but it is vital to our study. You don't need to memorize this information, just refer back to it to put Daniel into context.

The Babylonian Empire is first on our list, because it surrounds the Book of Daniel. Babylon started giving Jerusalem problems around B.C. 605, thus beginning the Babylonian Captivity. They sieged Jerusalem and forced the Jews to pay tribute. But as the Book of Jeremiah records, the Jews thought God would defend them, so they resisted. God was, in fact, using Babylon as an instrument of judgment against Jerusalem. Since the Jews resisted, Babylon returned several times to subdue them.

During Nebuchadnezzar's reign, Babylon implemented a policy of deportations to help quell the population. This was a normal practice in the ancient world. When an invading empire conquered a new land, they would take many of the local inhabitants and disperse them around the empire. If you decentralize a people, it makes it much harder for them to challenge your rule.

Babylon instituted 3 deportations against Jerusalem: B.C. 597, B.C. 587, and B.C. 582. Daniel was part of one of these deportations. His particular group was taken to the city of Babylon.

Our narrative centers around Jerusalem, but we need to look at the broader world around Jerusalem to get a clear context for Daniel's prophecies.

Around this time, the Medes were advancing through modern day Iran and eastern Turkey. At this point, the Medes had become a major power in the ancient world. In B.C. 612, they captured Nineveh (the capital of ancient Assyria), wiping away the remnants of the once great Assyrian Empire (the same empire that destroyed the northern kingdoms of Israel). Even though the Persians quickly conquered the Medes, the Medes will become important in our discussion of Daniel.

The Persians were originally part of Medes. But in B.C. 550, led by Cyrus the Great, the Persians rebelled and conquered the Medes. This was almost 50 years after the first deportation of Jews to Babylon.

Then, in B.C. 536, Cyrus conquered Babylon and allowed the Jews to return to their homeland. Thus ending the Babylonian Captivity. The Persians would rule much of the ancient world for several hundred years. It was under the Persians that Ezra and Nehemiah returned to Jerusalem to rebuild the Temple and Jerusalem.

Things didn't change much until B.C. 334 (200 years later), when Alexander the Great crossed into Persian territory. He quickly defeated the Persians in a series of battles and took over their territory. His empire annexed Jerusalem in B.C. 332. But Alexander died in B.C. 323, and his empire fractured.

The largest piece of his empire became known as the Seleucid Kingdom, which plays a leading role in Daniel's prophecies as well. During this time, a Seleucid king named Antiochus IV (ruled from B.C. 175 – 164) sacked Jerusalem and persecuted the Jews (which we will discuss in great depth later).

Rome enters the picture in B.C. 63, when they annexed Syria and the surrounding areas. Jesus was born under Roman rule, and the entire New Testament took place under the Roman Empire.

This may seem like a lot of random information, but these events lay an important foundation for our study of Daniel. Remember to refer back to this section as you read so that you have a framework upon which to understand Daniel.

Timeline of Ancient Empires

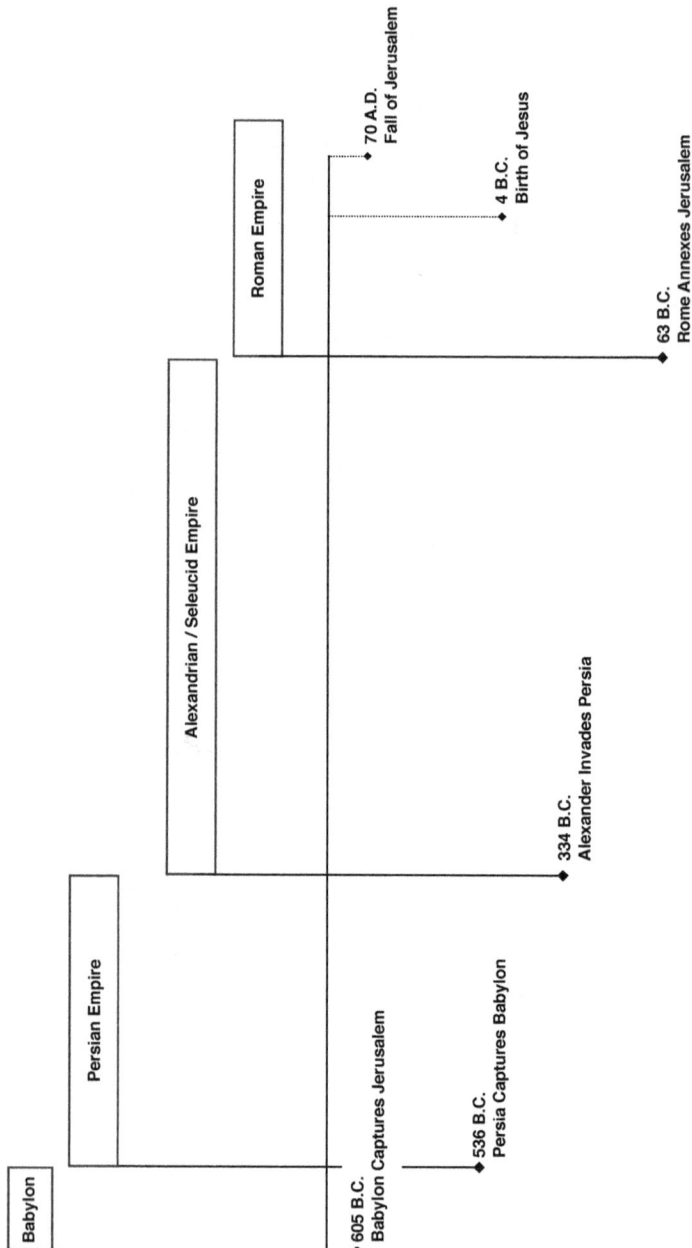

Babylon

Persian Empire

Alexandrian / Seleucid Empire

Roman Empire

605 B.C.
Babylon Captures Jerusalem

536 B.C.
Persia Captures Babylon

334 B.C.
Alexander Invades Persia

63 B.C.
Rome Annexes Jerusalem

4 B.C.
Birth of Jesus

70 A.D.
Fall of Jerusalem

Chapter 2

DANIEL 2: THE STATUE

Daniel 2 contains Nebuchadnezzar's vision of a statue (Nebuchadnezzar was the king who conquered Jerusalem and deported the Jews around his empire). Daniel has already been deported to Babylon and is among the king's spiritual advisors. Responding to Nebuchadnezzar's call, Daniel gives a supernatural revelation of the dream:

> "You, O king, were watching; and behold, a great image! ... This image's head was of fine gold, its chest and arms of silver, its belly and thighs of bronze, its legs of iron, its feet partly of iron and partly of clay. You watched while a stone was cut out without hands, which struck the image on its feet of iron and clay, and broke them in pieces. Then the iron, the clay, the bronze, the silver, and the gold were crushed together, and became like chaff from the summer threshing floors; the wind carried them away so that no trace of them was found. And the stone that struck the image became a great mountain and filled the whole earth." [54]

---

54. Daniel 2:31-35

In his dream, Nebuchadnezzar sees a statue of a man. It has a gold head, silver abdomen, bronze thighs, iron legs, and its feet are made of iron and clay. Then a stone was cut from the earth without the use of hands. That stone was then thrown at the feet of the statue. The statue collapsed and the stone grew into a mountain that consumed the whole earth. After recounting the dream to Nebuchadnezzar, Daniel interprets the dream:

> "This is the dream… You, O king, are a king of kings… you are this head of gold. But after you shall arise another kingdom inferior to yours; then another, a third kingdom of bronze, which shall rule over all the earth. And the fourth kingdom shall be as strong as iron, inasmuch as iron breaks in pieces and shatters everything; and like iron that crushes, that kingdom will break in pieces and crush all the others. Whereas you saw the feet and toes, partly of potter's clay and partly of iron, the kingdom shall be divided; yet the strength of the iron shall be in it, just as you saw the iron mixed with ceramic clay. And as the toes of the feet were partly of iron and partly of clay, so the kingdom shall be partly strong and partly fragile. As you saw iron mixed with ceramic clay, they will mingle with the seed of men; but they will not adhere to one another, just as iron does not mix with clay."[55]

Daniel reveals to Nebuchadnezzar that the different metals represented different kingdoms. He tells the king that Babylon was the head made of gold. He then goes on to talk about the following kingdoms:

---

55. Daniel 3:35-44

"And in the days of these kings the God of heaven will set up a kingdom which shall never be destroyed; and the kingdom shall not be left to other people; it shall break in pieces and consume all these kingdoms, and it shall stand forever. Inasmuch as you saw that the stone was cut out of the mountain without hands, and that it broke in pieces the iron, the bronze, the clay, the silver, and the gold—the great God has made known to the king what will come to pass after this. The dream is certain, and its interpretation is sure."[56]

Both preterists and futurists agree that the rock is Jesus. They agree that He will come, destroy the kingdoms in this vision, and set up an eternal Kingdom. They differ on the identity of the kingdoms and when this happens.

Futurists believe that the kingdoms go as such: Babylon, Medo-Persia, Greece, Rome, and a Neo-Roman Empire that has yet to form. This "Neo-Roman Empire" is the kingdom of the Antichrist.

They identify the iron legs of the statue as the original Roman Empire. Daniel says the iron kingdom is "like iron that crushes," and Rome conquered the entire civilized world. That leaves the final kingdom that was made of iron mixed with clay. So, futurists are looking for a kingdom that resembles the Roman Empire, but different because it was mixed with clay. This is why many Christians are suspicious of the United Nations, or the European Union, or the Roman Catholic Church. They all resemble the Roman Empire in some way.

---

56. Daniel 2:44-45

Yet, we can see a different flow of events if we carefully analyze Daniels interpretation and compare it to events in history.

Futurist View of Daniel's Statue

Statue Composition	Corresponding Kingdom
Gold	**Babylonian Empire** (626 B.C. – 536 B.C.)
Silver	**Medo-Persian Empire** (536 B.C. – 330 B.C.)
Bronze	**Alexandrian / Seleucid Empire** (336 B.C. – 63 B.C.)
Iron	**Roman Republic / Empire** (509 B.C. - 476 A.D.)
Prophetic Gap	
Iron & Clay	**Future Kingdom of the Antichrist** (Soon – ?)

Daniel states that the second empire would be inferior to Babylon. But if we go with the futurist understanding of the kingdoms, the second kingdom would be the Medo-Persian Empire. The Medo-Persian empire was anything but inferior to Babylon. It was far bigger and more powerful.

But we call it "Medo-Persian" because Persia absorbed a smaller kingdom on its rise to power called Medes. The Medes Empire was bigger in size to Babylon, but not as powerful. In fact, many histories don't discuss the Medes Empire on it own because of its insignificance. They lump it in with the Persian Empire. But the Medes Empire held preeminence for sixty years before Persia conquered it.

Persia then went on to be the most powerful empire the world had ever seen. This fits with Daniel because he said that the third empire would "conquer the whole world." Thus, it makes more sense that the kingdom after Babylon were the Medes, and that the third kingdom was Persia.

According to Daniel, the fourth kingdom was like iron because it crushed all the other kingdoms to pieces. Rome seems to be the obvious choice for this kingdom. But the next empire to rise in history was Macedonia, led by Alexander the Great. Alexander's conquests were the largest in history and he seemed unstoppable.

Other kingdoms expanded over the course of several kings, spanning hundreds of years. But Alexander conquered most of the known world within twenty years. To the people of that time, this would have seemed superhuman.

You could say that he crushed all the other kingdoms under his feet. And he did it at lightening speeds.

Therefore, Alexander the Great's Empire fits the criteria for the fourth kingdom. This makes Rome the kingdom of iron and clay. And if true, this has profound repercussions on our timeline.

Preterist View of Daniel's Statue

Statue Composition	Corresponding Kingdom
Gold	**Babylonian Empire** (626 B.C. − 536 B.C.)
Silver	**Medes Empire** (612 B.C. − 550 B.C.)
Bronze	**Persian Empire** (550 B.C. − 330 B.C.)
Iron	**Alexandrian / Seleucid Empire** (336 B.C. - 323 A.D.)
Iron & Clay	**Roman Empire** (509 B.C. − 476 A.D.)

First off, Daniel doesn't say that there will be a gap between the fourth kingdom and the final kingdom. Much less a two thousand year gap. You have to read that into the text.

Daniel 2: The Statue

Daniel says that the final kingdom contained elements of Alexander's kingdom, but mixed with clay:

> "Whereas you saw the feet and toes, partly of potter's clay and partly of iron, the kingdom shall be divided; yet **the strength of the iron shall be in it**, just as you saw the iron mixed with ceramic clay. And as the toes of the feet were partly of iron and partly of clay, so the kingdom shall be **partly strong and partly fragile**. As you saw iron mixed with ceramic clay, they will **mingle with the seed of men**; but they will not adhere to one another, just as iron does not mix with clay."[57]

Daniel says that the final kingdom would have the strength of the fourth kingdom, but that "the seed of men" would weaken it.

Rome had all the strength of Alexander's Empire. It crushed all other kingdoms of the world underneath it. Yet it also suffered from a serious weakness: its emperors. They never formed a stable succession policy.

Often, when an emperor died, wars broke out to determine who would be the next emperor. Whole portions of the empire would rebel, and the new emperor would have to reconquering them.

Starting around A.D. 100, the Roman Empire began to experience decline. Though it would reach its largest size in A.D. 117, the empire could not support itself. The empire fought constant foreign wars, and imperial

---

57. Daniel 2:41-43, emphasis added.

assassinations became common. Starting in A.D. 186, there were 37 different emperors over the next 100 years–25 of whom were assassinated. The empire was just as massive and as strong as Alexander's empire, but it was internally fragile.

Emperors diverted money to wars and away from internal maintenance. This caused infrastructure to deteriorate. Water and food supplies dwindled as emperors pursued their political ambitions.

Due to famine and plague, the population size dropped. The army shrank because of the decline in population and was unable to maintain control over the empire.

Daniel said that the fifth kingdom would be "a divided kingdom," and Rome eventually split under its own weight. It split down the middle and formed two empires, both of which called themselves Rome. Starting around the end of the 4th century, barbarian groups pushed into the western empire. With a smaller military, Rome couldn't defend itself.

Daniel said that the stone would break the final kingdom into many pieces. Over time, the western Roman empire crumbled into nothing.

An empire as strong and powerful as Rome was undone by the political ambitions of a few men. Rome had the strength of the iron kingdom, but the "seed of men" weakened it.

The rock in Nebuchadnezzar's vision further anchors these events in the first century. In his dream, the rock grew to consume the whole world after destroying the fifth kingdom. Most scholars agree that the Rock is Jesus, which makes Rome the fifth Kingdom. In describing the final kingdom, Daniel says:

> "And in the days of these kings the God of heaven will set up a kingdom, which shall never be destroyed; and the kingdom shall not be left to other people; **it shall break in pieces and consume all these kingdoms, and it shall stand forever.**"[58]

God threw the rock at the fifth Kingdom. Jesus was born around B.C. 4, right in the middle of the Roman era.

Daniel says that the rock would establish a kingdom that destroyed all others, and that it would grow to consume the whole world. During His ministry, Jesus broke the powers of hell and commissioned His disciples to spread the Kingdom throughout the world.

At the beginning of Jesus' ministry, Satan had dominion of the planet. We know this because in Luke 4, Satan has power over all the kingdoms of the earth: "All this authority I will give You, and their glory; for this has been delivered to me, and I give it to whomever I wish."[59] He was able to offer the kingdoms to Jesus because He owned them.

But later, Jesus said that He took it back... two thousand years ago. After Jesus rose from the dead, He

---

58. Daniel 2:43-44, emphasis added

59. Luke 4:6-7

declared to His disciples: "All authority has been given to Me in heaven and on earth, therefore go and make disciples of all nations..."[60]

If Jesus has all authority in Heaven and on earth, then it means that Satan has none. Jesus' death and resurrection not only paid for our sins, but it took Satan's authority away. This is further corroborated in Colossians 2: "Having disarmed principalities and powers, He made a public spectacle of them, triumphing over them in it." [61] Jesus not only defeated Satan's kingdom, He made a public spectacle of him.

Jesus also established His own Kingdom. At the outset of His ministry, He announced the arrival of the Kingdom: "The time is fulfilled, and the Kingdom of God is at hand. Repent, and believe in the good news." [62] He was announcing that the Kingdom prophesied in the Old Testament was here. He also told Pilate that His Kingdom "was not of this world." [63] Instead of an earthly kingdom, it was a spiritual one. The Jews didn't have a concept for this, and asked Him about it:

"Now when He was asked by the Pharisees when the kingdom of God would come, He answered them and said,

60. Matthew 28:18

61. Colossians 2:15

62. Mark 1:15. Also see: Matthew 4:12–17; Luke 4:14, 15.

63. John 18:36

Daniel 2: The Statue

'The kingdom of God does not come with observation; nor will they say, 'See here!' or 'See there!' For indeed, the kingdom of God is within you.'" [64]

Many Christians are expecting a physical Kingdom of God just like the Pharisees. They wonder at how Jesus could have brought the Kingdom two thousand years ago. But Jesus said that the Kingdom is not something that you can see. It is not a country that has specific boundaries on a map. It is within us.

Jesus taught us to pray: "Our Father in Heaven, Hallowed be Your name. Your Kingdom come, Your will be done on Earth as it is in Heaven." [65] He taught us to pray that His Kingdom would advance on earth.

Some think that the Kingdom of God will come all at once in the second coming. But Daniel tells us that it will grow over time: "And the stone that struck the image became a great mountain and filled the whole earth." [66]

Furthermore, Jesus established the Kingdom two thousand years ago by His own words. He said: "Assuredly, I say to you that there are some standing here who will not taste death till they see the Kingdom of God present with power." [67] Jesus was talking to a group of people

---

64. Luke 17:20-21

65. Matthew 6:9,10

66. Daniel 2:35

67. Mark 9:1

alive two thousand years ago. He said that they would see the Kingdom before they died (or at least some of them). This means that the Kingdom of God had to have been established two thousand years ago.

It did not come all at once. He said it would come like a mustard seed. It would be tiny. But as it grew it would consume the whole earth. And as the Kingdom (Christianity) grew, it destroyed the Roman empire.

There hasn't been an empire like Rome since. Jesus' Kingdom started small (only 12 men) but it grew to consume the whole of the ancient world.

Today, more than two billion people call themselves Christian. And those numbers continue to grow. Lisa Ling, a well-known reporter in the United States, said that Christianity was the fastest growing religion in the United States.[68] Outside of the United States, people estimate that twenty-five thousand people come to Jesus every day in China. Even the Muslim world recognizes it is in danger of losing Africa to Christianity. They estimate that sixteen thousand Muslims in Africa come to Jesus every day.[69] We are in a state of worldwide revival.

---

68. Lisa Ling, "Our America with Lisa Ling: Faith Healers," Season 1, Episode 1 (Los Angeles, CA: Oprah Winfrey Network: OWN, February 2011).

69. Web-Archive of Al-Jazeera Interview, "Interview with Sheikh Ahmed Al Katani on the Christianization of Africa," (December 12, 2012): "In Africa... every hour 667 Muslims convert to Christianity, 16,000 every day, 6 million each year..."

Jesus was born into a kingdom that had the strength of iron, but weakened by clay. He established His Kingdom and ascended to the right hand of the Father. Rome crumbled under the weakness of its emperors and fell apart. Whereas God's Kingdom continues to grow as it marches on to consume the whole world. Just like Daniel predicted.

Chapter 3

DANIEL 7: THE LITTLE HORN

Daniel 7 contains the Vision of the Four Beasts. His vision consists of four beasts rising out of the "Great Sea" that had power over the world. Then, with the rise of the fourth beast, God establishes a Kingdom that ends the dominion of the other beasts. This should sound familiar to the vision in Chapter 2. They are discussing the same events from a different perspective. Here is the vision:

"Daniel spoke, saying, 'I saw in my vision by night, and behold, the four winds of heaven were stirring up the Great Sea. And four great beasts came up from the sea, each different from the other. The first was like a lion, and had eagle's wings. I watched till its wings were plucked off; and it was lifted up from the earth and made to stand on two feet like a man, and a man's heart was given to it.

"And suddenly another beast, a second, like a bear. It was raised up on one side, and had three ribs in its mouth between its teeth. And they said thus to it: 'Arise, devour much flesh!'

"After this I looked, and there was another, like a leopard, which had on its back four wings of a bird. The beast also had four heads, and dominion was given to it.

"After this I saw in the night visions, and behold, a fourth beast, dreadful and terrible, exceedingly strong. It had huge iron teeth; it was devouring, breaking in pieces, and trampling the residue with its feet. It was different from all the beasts that were before it, and it had ten horns. I was considering the horns, and there was another horn, a little one, coming up among them, before whom three of the first horns were plucked out by the roots. And there, in this horn, were eyes like the eyes of a man, and a mouth speaking pompous words."[70]

Daniel has a vision in a dream. He does not see four literal beasts. Nor does he see four natural kings or kingdoms. He is witnessing demonic powers that are influencing the natural world. Each one has its own unique authority and ugliness.[71] But they are not actual kingdoms. They are the spiritual principalities that empower natural kingdoms.

Daniel says that these powers are given authority to rule and destroy much flesh. The fourth beast is far more powerful than the others and produces a king that blasphemes God.

---

70. Daniel 7:2-8

71. Daniel 7:5

This fourth beast produced ten horns, three of which were "plucked out by the roots," after which a little horn rose "among" them. Gabriel tells us that these horns represent kings. So, what does this vision depict?

Many Christian teachers believe that the little horn is the Antichrist in Satan's future kingdom.

This passage tells us that this king will persecute the "saints." This leads many to believe that the Antichrist will persecute the Church before Jesus returns. Or that he will persecute the Jews during the tribulation.

But to arrive at those conclusions, you have to take these passages out of context. When we study the context and the history around Daniel, we will see a different interpretation.

The four beasts are the spiritual powers that influenced the four kingdoms of Babylonia, Medes, Persia, and Macedonia/Rome. The "little horn" is a Seleucid king named Antiochus Epiphanes (or Antiochus IV) who persecuted the Jews. The Kingdom established at the end of this passage is not a future fulfillment of eternity. It is the Kingdom Jesus ushered in two thousand years ago, just like the Kingdom in Daniel 2.

First, we can ground these kingdoms in history. Verse 23 says that the fourth beast "shall devour the whole earth, trample it and break it in pieces." Daniel 2 used similar language to describe Alexander the Great's empire and the Roman Empire.

Gabriel tells us that the 11 horns Daniel sees represent

kings.[72] The description of these kings bears a striking similarity to the first eleven kings of Alexander's empire.

After his death, the Seleucid Empire succeeded Alexander's. It was Greek and controlled most of the territory Alexander had conquered, and established its capital in Babylon. For all intense and purposes, it was the same empire.

Daniel 2 says this fourth beast had "10 horns," three of which were "plucked out by the roots," and that a little horn rose "among" them. Gabriel tells us that these horns represented kings. Here are the first eleven kings of Alexander's Empire:

1. Alexander the Great
2. Seleucus I Nicator
3. Antiochus I Soter
4. Antiochus II Theos
5. Seleucus II Callinicus
6. Seleucus III Ceraunus
7. Antiochus III the Great
8. Seleucus IV Philopator (assassinated)
9. Heliodorus (assassinated)
10. Seleucus IV's infant son Antiochus (assassinated)
11. Antiochus IV Epiphanes

This list of kings corresponds with the horns described in Daniel 7. Before Antiochus rose to power, the previous

---

72. Daniel 7:24

three kings were assassinated–or "plucked out by the roots." Gabriel goes on to tell us more about Antiochus (the little horn):

> "He [the little horn] shall speak pompous words
>   against the Most High,
> Shall persecute the saints of the Most High,
> And shall intend to change times and law.
> Then the saints shall be given into his hand
> For a time and times and half a time." [73]

This passage tells us that the eleventh king will do several things. He will blaspheme God. He will persecute God's people. And He will attempt to change the religious customs and laws of God's people. Antiochus IV did all these things.

In B.C. 168, Antiochus sacked Jerusalem. He slaughtered thousands of Jews (the Jews were known as the "saints" at this point in history[74]).

He also thought that Jewish monotheism was strange and backwards. So, he tried to force Greek culture and values onto the Jews. He erected a statue of Zeus in the Temple. He forced the worship of the Greek gods. He outlawed monotheism. He halted the Jewish sacrificial system. And he forced them to sacrifice pork in the Temple. Thus, he "changed the times and laws."

---

73. Daniel 7:25

74. See 1st and 2nd Maccabees

This caused the Jews to rebel in B.C. 164. And though they saw some success in their revolt, they were never able to push Antiochus out of Jerusalem. Thus he was able to carry out these "reforms" for several years.

Antiochus fits the timeline of Daniel 7 (the eleventh king of this Kingdom) and the description of the eleventh king. He persecuted the Jews. He tried to change times and laws (their religious system). And the Jews "were given into his hand." But Daniel goes on:

> "But the court shall be seated,
> And they shall take away his dominion,
> To consume and destroy it forever.
> Then the kingdom and dominion,
> And the greatness of the kingdoms under the whole heaven,
> Shall be given to the people, the saints of the Most High.
> His kingdom is an everlasting kingdom,
> And all dominions shall serve and obey Him."[75]

These verses tell us that the eleventh king's authority will be destroyed. Then God will give authority over all the kingdoms of the earth to His people. Daniel goes on:

> "Then to Him was given dominion and glory
> and a kingdom,
> That all peoples, nations, and languages
> should serve Him.
> His dominion is an everlasting dominion,

---

75. Daniel 7:26-27

Which shall not pass away,
And His kingdom the one
Which shall not be destroyed."[76]

Daniel 7 tells us that the establishment of God's Kingdom is tied to the destruction of the fourth beast. It also says that all authority over the earth will be given to the saints. This happened two thousand years ago with Jesus' death, resurrection, and the Great Commission.

The Greco-Roman Empire

Some might notice that the time gap between Antiochus IV and Jesus' birth was around 150 years. This may raise some red flags. Some may also notice that we jumped from the Seleucid Empire (Antiochus) to the Roman Empire (Jesus). To understand how these events line up, we need to look at the fourth beast and correlate it to the vision in Daniel 2.

We don't know how spiritual principalities always manifest in the natural. It is possible that one of Daniel's beasts could have influenced multiple kingdoms. In fact, Daniel 2 illustrates that one spirit did influenced two kingdoms.

The fourth and fifth kingdoms in Daniel 2 both had iron in them. But the fifth kingdom also contained clay. Since both kingdoms had iron in them, it is reasonable to conclude that the same spirit inspired them both. Rome

76. Daniel 7: 14

derived its power from the same principality that inspired the Macedonian Empire (iron). The fourth beast in Daniel 7 represents the spirit behind the Seleucid/Greek and Roman Empires.

The Statue and The Beasts

Daniel 2 Statue	Daniel 7 Beasts	Corresponding Kingdom
Gold	**First Beast** Lion with Wings	**Babylonian Empire** (626 B.C. – 536 B.C.)
Silver	**Second Beast** Bear the Consumed Flesh	**Medes Empire** (612 B.C. – 550 B.C.)
Bronze	**Third Beast** Four Headed Leopard	**Persian Empire** (550 B.C. – 330 B.C.)
Iron	**Fourth Beast** Iron Teeth with Ten Horns	**Alexandrian / Seleucid Empire** (336 B.C. - 323 A.D.)
Iron & Clay		**Roman Empire** (509 B.C. – 476 A.D.)

This makes even more sense when we look at Greek and Roman cultures. Babylon, Persia, and Greece all had distinct cultures. They had different gods, customs, and social structures. The differences in their religious beliefs reveal separate spiritual influences.[77] But Daniel tells us that the fourth beast was unique when compared to the others.[78] One of these differences may have been its ability to influence multiple natural kingdoms.

Though the first three kingdoms had different cultures, Romans adopted Greek culture:

"Greek influence on Rome dated from the beginning of the city's history and had become an integral part of Roman culture by the time Rome intervened in the affairs of the Hellenistic east... Roman aristocrats routinely acquired a Greek education... Rome's gods and myths had been recast in terms of Greek mythology. Latin writers constantly echoed their Greek predecessors, so that a work like Virgil's *Aeneid*, Rome's national epic, has to be read against the background of the *Iliad* and the *Odyssey*..."[79]

The Romans incorporated many aspects of Greek customs into their own, including their gods. The Romans even

77. It is true that all ancient societies, except for the Hebrews, were polytheistic and syncretistic in nature. So some may argue that even though their gods had different names, they were essentially the same religion. But this would be a gross oversimplification. Just because one polytheistic faith could make room for another set of gods and traditions does not mean that they were the same. Even a cursory study of ancient religious traditions would reveal stark differences between them.

78. Daniel 7:7

79. Sarah B. Pomeroy and others, *Ancient Greece: A Political, Social, and Cultural History, 2nd Edition* (New York, NY: Oxford University Press, 2008), 508.

based their republican government upon the democratic ideals of the Greeks. The Roman and Grecian cultures became so intertwined that many refer to it as the Greco-Roman culture.

Also, "while Greeks and Greek culture prospered under Roman rule, the same was not true of the non-Greek cultures of Egypt and the Near East…".[80] Meaning, that while Rome exalted Grecian culture, they devalued all others. And the only way a Roman could become more than a commoner was by receiving a Greek education.[81]

It seems safe to conclude that the same spirit, the fourth beast, inspired both kingdoms. The Romans believed in the same gods as the Greeks. They practiced similar religious practices as the Greeks. They held similar moral standards. They structured their societies in a similar fashion. They used a Greek education system. And they had the conquering power of the Macedonian Empire.

All of these ancient empires were evil and powerful. But after the Roman Empire collapsed, we don't see another one like them. The demonic forces behind them lost their dominion on the planet.

If we believe that these events have yet to happen, then it means that Satan still has power, dominion, and a kingdom. But he can't. Jesus stated two thousand years ago that He had all authority, leaving Satan with none.

---

80. Pomeroy, 509.

81. Pomeroy, 509.

This means that Satan's kingdom was destroyed around A.D. 30. This forces us to conclude that Daniel 7 must have taken place at the same time.

Some might wonder why evil persists if Jesus took Satan's kingdom from him two thousand years ago. Daniel 7:12 states that the three remaining beasts were allowed to persist on the earth for a "season and a time." This means they are still here, but without their kingdoms. Demonic powers are still present in the world, but they have lost their authority. The only authority Satan now maintains is his ability to deceive us. If he, or his demons, can convince us to believe a lie, our faith in that lie will empower it. But without our consent, they have no authority.

Not only did Jesus destroy Satan's kingdom, but He gave us control of His own Kingdom: "He sent them to preach the kingdom of God and to heal the sick," (Luke 9:2). "He who believes in Me, the works that I do he will do also; and greater works than these he will do," (John 14:12). "All things that the Father has are Mine. Therefore I said that [the Holy Spirit] will take what is Mine and give it to you," (John 16:15).

Daniel 7 states this would happen: "Then the kingdom and dominion, and the greatness of the kingdoms under the whole heaven shall be given to the people, the saints of the Most High."[82]

Everything in Daniel 7 lines up with events that

---

82. Daniel 7:26

occurred two thousand years ago. The vision in Daniel 7 was about Antiochus IV and his persecution of the saints. It was also about the demonic powers that inspired the evil kingdoms leading up to Jesus' grand coup d'état.

Chapter 4

THE 70TH WEEK OF DANIEL

The 70th week of Daniel has caused a lot of speculation amongst Christians. People have interpreted Daniel chapter 9 thousands of times in a thousand different ways. Yet, like the other chapters in Daniel we have studied, these events do not pertain to our future.

At the beginning of chapter 9, we see Daniel praying for the redemption of God's people. He is praying for God to end the Babylonian captivity.

In the middle of this prayer, Gabriel appears before him. Gabriel tells Daniel that God sent him to answer Daniel's prayers and give him "skill to understand." Gabriel is answering Daniel's prayers about the Jews in Babylon. He is not discussing the end of the world. Here is what he says:

> "Seventy weeks are determined
> For your people and for your holy city,

To finish the transgression,
To make an end of sins,
To make reconciliation for iniquity,
To bring in everlasting righteousness,
To seal up vision and prophecy,
And to anoint the Most Holy.
"Know therefore and understand,
That from the going forth of the command
To restore and build Jerusalem
Until Messiah the Prince,
There shall be seven weeks and sixty-two weeks;
The street shall be built again, and the wall,
Even in troublesome times.
"And after the sixty-two weeks
Messiah shall be cut off, but not for Himself;
And the people of the prince who is to come
Shall destroy the city and the sanctuary.
The end of it shall be with a flood,
And till the end of the war desolations are determined.
Then he shall confirm a covenant with many for one week;
But in the middle of the week
He shall bring an end to sacrifice and offering.
And on the wing of abominations shall be one who makes desolate,
Even until the consummation, which is determined,
Is poured out on the desolate."[83]

Gabriel gives Daniel an outline of Israel's future. He comforts Daniel by telling him that the Jews will have a time of God's favor. They will return to Jerusalem. They will rebuild their city and their Temple. But he

---

83. Daniel 9:24-27

goes on to give Daniel an even bigger picture of God's plan. He says that the Messiah will come. But that God will destroy Jerusalem in judgment.

Many Christians believe these events will unfold in our future. They think there will be a time when God's favor returns to Israel where He elevates them to a place of authority in the world. They believe that the Jews will return to their homeland. They will rebuild their Temple. And they will resume their sacrificial system. Thus, many Christians believe we are in the final hours because the U.N. reconstituted Israel in the late 1940s. They see this as the first sign that prophecy is coming to pass.

But, this does not take the history of Israel into consideration. All these things already happened a long time ago. The Jews did return home. They rebuilt their temple. They restored their sacrificial system. They had a period of favor with God and the world. Then they were judged, and Jerusalem was destroyed. Just like Daniel 9 predicted. There is no need to look to the future. This prophecy has already come to pass.

Undertanding Daniel 9

Both preterists and futurists believe that the 70 weeks of Daniel represents 490 years.[84] Each week equaling 7

---

84. It is common in apocalyptic literature for days to mean years, as we will see in Revelation. Therefore, with 7 days in a week, the 70 weeks represented 490 years (7 days times 70 weeks).

years. Gabriel states that there will be 69 weeks (483 years) between the decree to rebuild Jerusalem and the arrival of the Messiah:

> "Know therefore and understand,
> That from the going forth of the command
> To restore and build Jerusalem
> Until Messiah the Prince,
> There shall be seven weeks and sixty-two weeks;
> The street shall be built again, and the wall,
> Even in troublesome times."[85]

If we do some math, we find a startling correlation between these numbers and historical events. In B.C. 457, Artexerxes, the king of Persia decreed that Jerusalem should be rebuilt. [86] The decree went out. According to Daniel, this means that the Messiah should have arrived 483 years later.

Most scholars believe that Jesus was born in B.C. 4, meaning that He started His ministry in A.D. 27—*483 years after Artexerxes' decree*. This is exactly what Daniel predicted hundreds of years earlier.

Both preterists and futurist recognize the accuracy of

---

85. Daniel 9:25

86. Nehemiah tells us that the city was rebuilt surrounded by enemies conspiring against them (Nehemiah 4,6), so much so that he even tells us they worked with one hand to rebuild the walls and had a spear in the other to fight off attackers – meaning it was rebuilt "even in troublesome times" – just as Gabriel said.

this passage. But, many Christians postpone the seventieth week to some point in our future. They believe we currently live in the space between the 69th and the 70th weeks. In this view, the arrival of the Antichrist will mark the beginning of the 70th week:

> "Then he shall confirm a covenant with many for one
>   week;
> But in the middle of the week
> He shall bring an end to sacrifice and offering."[87]

Many people believe that the "he" in this passage is the Antichrist. They believe he will make a covenant with the Jews, promising them peace and safety.

69 Weeks of Daniel

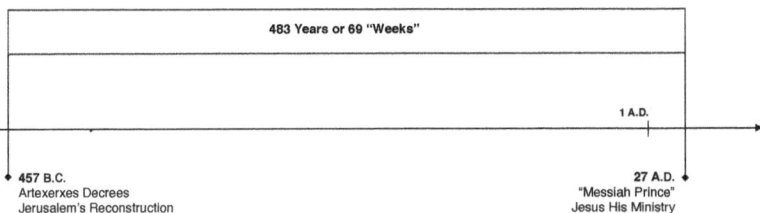

| 483 Years or 69 "Weeks" | 1 A.D. |

457 B.C.
Artexerxes Decrees
Jerusalem's Reconstruction

27 A.D.
"Messiah Prince"
Jesus His Ministry

---

87. Daniel 9:27

But three and a half years later he will break that promise and put an end to the sacrificial system. After this, he will cause the world to blaspheme against God and His people. At this point, God will pour out His final judgment against the world.

This is why many Christians are waiting for the Jews to rebuild the Temple. For them, this will signal the rise of the Antichrist.

Many people have suggested that the U.N. is the Antichrist's "kingdom." This is because the U.N. formed and enforced Israel's reconstitution. But let's take a different look at this passage.

First, Gabriel does not imply a gap between the 69th and 70th weeks. You have to read that into the text.

Secondly, these predictions line up with first century events. Gabriel states that the purpose of the 70 weeks are "... to finish the transgression, to make an end of sins, to make reconciliation for iniquity, to bring in everlasting righteousness." When were transgressions finished? When were sins ended? When was iniquity reconciled? When was everlasting righteousness bestowed?

This all happened two thousand years ago with the atonement of Jesus on the cross. God said that after 70 weeks He would establish everlasting righteousness. If we think the 70th week is yet to come, then we have to postpone a part of the work of the cross. But Jesus said, "It is finished." God achieved 100% atonement two thousand years ago.

Also, this passage never makes reference to the

Antichrist. The only person mentioned is the Messiah. Thus, the "he" in this passage must refer to the Messiah. Otherwise the grammar wouldn't make any sense. The author would have introduced a new character with an impersonal pronoun without identifying them.

Preterist View of the 70th Week

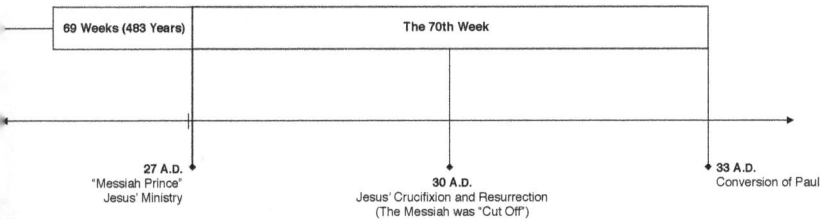

69 Weeks (483 Years)	The 70th Week

27 A.D.
"Messiah Prince"
Jesus' Ministry

30 A.D.
Jesus' Crucifixion and Resurrection
(The Messiah was "Cut Off")

33 A.D.
Conversion of Paul

Furthermore, Jesus fits the description better than the Antichrist. Gabriel says that "And after the sixty-two weeks [which is actually the 69th week], Messiah shall be cut off, but not for Himself." "Shall be cut off" can also mean to "suffer the death penalty."[88] Gabriel is saying that the death of the Messiah will mark the seventieth week. And Jesus did not die "for Himself," but for us.[89]

---

88. Daniel 9:26

89. 1 Peter 2:21

Gabriel goes on to say that the Messiah will confirm a covenant for one week. And then in the middle of that week He will bring an end to the sacrificial system.

From 27 A.D. to 33 A.D. (seven years) Jesus and His disciples only preached the gospel of the kingdom to the Jews. Jesus only revealed the Kingdom to the Jews (three and a half years).[90] Then after His death and resurrection, the disciples stayed in Jerusalem to preach. Acts tells us that they didn't leave even in the face of persecution:

> "At that time a great persecution arose against the Church which was at Jerusalem; and they were all scattered throughout the regions of Judea and Samaria, *except the apostles*."[91]

Many scholars believe there were three and a half years between Jesus' resurrection and the conversion of Paul. Paul was the first apostle to preach the Kingdom to the gentiles. This means that the Jews had exclusive access to the Kingdom of God for seven years.

Then Gabriel said, "But in the middle of the week He shall bring an end to sacrifice and offering." In the middle of that week (three and a half years) Jesus put an end to the sacrificial system. The Book of Hebrews states that the sacrificial system was a type of Jesus' atonement. Once He died and rose again, there was no need for a

---

90. Matthew 15:21-28

91. Acts 8:1

sacrifice. He was the ultimate sacrifice. Even though the Jews kept doing sacrifices for forty more years, there was no need. Thus, He put an end to the sacrificial system in the middle of this "week."

So, for three and a half years the Jews had the messiah teaching in their midst. He was "cut off" (killed). He made a new covenant with His people (the New Covenant). Subsequently, He put an end to the sacrificial system. Then, for three and a half more years, the disciples continued to preach the Kingdom to the Jews. But once this seven-year period was over, God opened the gospel to the rest of the world. At this point, the consummation of the 70 weeks occurred:

> "And the people of the prince who is to come
> Shall destroy the city and the sanctuary.
> The end of it shall be with a flood,
> And till the end of the war desolations are determined...
> And on the wing of abominations shall be one who makes desolate,
> Even until the consummation, which is determined,
> Is poured out on the desolate." [92]

God started a new covenant with a new people through Jesus. But Jerusalem (the sign of God's old covenant) still stood. Within one generation of these events, Jerusalem was destroyed (A.D. 70). This was the final blow to Judaism. The city was leveled. The Temple was burned to the

---

92. Daniel 9:26-27

ground. The sacrificial system formally ended (without a Temple, you can't do sacrifices). And it hasn't returned to this day. The Jews were banished from their homeland and scattered all over the world. Jerusalem and Judaism were left "desolate."

The seventy weeks of Daniel started when Artexerxes decreed the reconstruction of Jerusalem. And they ended when Peter and Paul started preaching amongst the gentiles. There is no need to look for these events in our future. They already occurred.

Chapter 12

SHUT UP THESE WORDS

There's one more verse that anchors these prophecies in the first century:

> "But you, Daniel, shut up the words, and seal the book until the time of the end." (Daniel 12:4)

At the end of Daniel, an angel tells Daniel to seal his records of all his prophetic visions. He is to seal them until right before the "end of the time" (Note: that the angel does not say the "end of time," but the "end of *the* time"). This poses a problem for futurism because the Book of Daniel has been "unsealed" for about 2,160 years.

Daniel doesn't appear in history until somewhere around B.C. 200–160. Daniel lived in the 500s BC, 300-340 years before any record of it appears in history. Some scholars argue that this means Daniel didn't write the book. They believe someone else wrote it later in Daniel's name. But it doesn't mean that.

Daniel followed his directions. He left the book with a group of disciples. He instructed them to keep Daniel secret until the appropriate time. Daniel appears between B.C. 200 – 160, which is right before Antiochus IV arrived. The Book of Daniel was a warning about Antiochus and the coming end of the age.

Furthermore, Daniel 12 anchors these events before the destruction of Jerusalem:

> "And one said to the man clothed in linen, who was above the waters of the river, **'How long shall the fulfillment of these wonders be?'** Then I heard the man clothed in linen, who was above the waters of the river, when he held up his right hand and his left hand to heaven, and swore by Him who lives forever, that it shall be for a time, times, and half a time; and **when the power of the holy people has been completely shattered, all these things shall be finished.**"[93]

One of the angels Daniel sees asks when these prophecies will come to pass. The other angel says that it will happen "when the power of the holy people has been completely shattered." Who are the "holy people"? Throughout the Book of Daniel, the saints and the "holy people" were the Jews. When was their power "shattered"? When Jesus came and did away with the Old Covenant. Then God destroyed their city with the Roman army. This anchors these events in the first century. Not our future.

---

93. Daniel 12:6-7, emphasis added.

Chapter 13

END OF THE AGE:
JERUSALEM'S FALL

To understand the apocalyptic passages in Scripture, we need to see how the Jews understood them. When we do that, will see that the Jews were not expecting the end of the world. They were expecting the "end of the age," which is very different.

Over the course of centuries, Jews began to associate the coming of their Messiah as the "end of the age." Nowhere in the Old Testament can you find a Jewish concept of the end of the world. To them, the "end of the age" would establish Israel as the preeminent power in the world. The world wouldn't end, but the age of gentile rule would.[94]

---

94. N.T. Wright, *The New Testament and the Kingdom of God* (Minneapolis, MN: Fortress Press, 1992), 284-286.

By the first century, the Jews still felt in exile from God, and they were waiting for that to change. They were expecting God to exalt them once again.

The Jews had been under the control of other kingdoms since the Babylonian Captivity. Except for a brief period just after Antiochus IV, they never again ruled themselves. Before Babylon conquered them, they were sovereign. And even though Babylon had allowed them to return to Jerusalem, gentile kingdoms still ruled over them for hundreds of years. We can tell that the Jews still thought they were in exile in Nehemiah's time:

> "Here we are, servants today!
> And the land that You gave to our fathers,
> To eat its fruit and its bounty,
> Here we are, servants in it!
> And it yields much increase to the kings
> You have set over us,
> Because of our sins;
> Also they have dominion over our bodies and our
>   cattle
> At their pleasure;
> And we are in great distress." [95]

Even though the Jews had returned to the Promised Land, they were still under the bondage of the gentile kings. This meant that the prophetic promises of Isaiah, Daniel, and other Old Testament authors for a Messiah and a new age had not yet come to pass. The Jews looked for God

---

95. Nehemiah 9:36-37

to fulfill these promises. Because of the timetable laid out in Daniel (see previous chapters), by the first century the Jews were in fervent expectation of God to restore Israel before the nations.

Furthermore, even though the Jews had rebuilt the Temple, they hadn't seen a return of the presence of God *in the Temple*. When Solomon first built the Temple, the presence of God descended onto it: "And it came to pass, when the priests came out of the holy place, that the cloud filled the house of the LORD, so that the priests could not continue ministering because of the cloud; for the glory of the LORD filled the house of the LORD."[96] This same cloud of God's presence left the Temple in Ezekiel 10:18. It signified Jerusalem's imminent judgment via Babylon. And it never returned.

Even after the Jews returned to their city and rebuilt the Temple, God's presence hadn't returned. This was still an expected hope. And until it happened, they saw themselves in exile.

Not only were the Jews expecting God to redeem them, they were expecting God to vindicate them in a dramatic way.

The persecution of Antiochus IV had been severe. But the Jews rebelled and saw success. Even though Antiochus never lost control of Jerusalem, he did lose the surrounding areas. Then, after Antiochus' death, the Seleucid kings retreated. To the Jews this was a huge

96. 1 Kings 8:10-11

victory. For a brief moment they were again sovereign. But their sovereignty was short lived. Rome annexed them.

N.T. Wright, a modern day biblical scholar, explains how the success of the Maccabean Revolt gave the Jews a dangerous precedent for how they thought God would redeem them:

> "The Maccabean revolt became classic and formative in the same way as the exodus and the other great events of Israel's history. It powerfully reinforced the basic Jewish worldview: when the tyrants rage, the one who dwells in the heaven will laugh at them in scorn. YHWH had vindicated his name, his land, his law-and his people."[97]

This laid a dangerous seed in their minds. If they resisted the gentiles, God would intervene and rescue them. Yet, even though the Maccabean Revolt pushed out the gentiles, it did not fulfill the exuberant expectations of the Kingdom of God.

Thus, many Jews used the Maccabean Revolt as a model for what was to come. This set the stage for the revolt against the Romans in A.D. 66 and the "end of the age."

The Jews were not just expecting God to restore His people. They were expecting a glorious age when all the nations of the earth served and recognized Israel's preeminence. The Messiah would usher in the age foretold by the Prophets. This was the "end of the age."

---

97. Wright, 159.

The Jews were feverishly expecting a Davidic king to rise, overthrow Rome, and usher in the Kingdom of God.

This Jewish expectation was so strong, that non-Jews even knew about it. Tacitus, a Roman historian, said this about the Jews:

"In most there was a firm persuasion, that in the ancient records of their priests was contained a prediction of how at this very time [the first century] the East was to grow powerful, and rulers, coming from Judaea, were to acquire universal empire."[98]

This is why Herod was afraid when the magi announced Jesus' birth. If the Jews thought their King had come, He knew they would rebel and he would lose his kingdom.

Scripture shows that even the disciples expected the Messiah to bring an earthly Kingdom, not the end of the world. This is why the disciples could not understand why Jesus had to die for their sins. That was outside of their paradigm for the "end of the age." For example, look at Luke 18:31-34:

"Then He took the twelve aside and said to them, 'Behold, we are going up to Jerusalem, and all things that are written by the prophets concerning the Son of Man will be accomplished. For He will be delivered to the Gentiles and will be mocked and insulted and spit upon. They will scourge Him and kill Him. And the third day He will rise again.'

---

98. Tacitus, *Histories*, trans. The Church and Brodribb (Macmillan, London: 1877), 5.13.

"But they understood none of these things; this saying
was hidden from them, and they did not know the things
which were spoken." [99]

How was the Messiah supposed to restore Israel, yet be
scourged and killed? Even after His death and resurrection they didn't get it. In Luke 24 we continue to see
this confusion.

After Jesus' resurrection, He appeared to two disciples,
yet they did not recognize Him. They began to tell Jesus
that they didn't understand what had happened over the
last several days:

"The things concerning Jesus of Nazareth, who was a
Prophet mighty in deed and word before God and all the
people, and how the chief priests and our rulers delivered Him to be condemned to death, and crucified Him.
**But we were hoping that it was He who was going to
redeem Israel.**"[100]

They did not understand that Israel's redemption would
come from the atonement. Otherwise they would have
understood why Jesus had to die. Their expectations of
the Messiah did not line up with what Jesus did. And
they were confused.

Stranger yet, the disciples still didn't understand His
mission at the Great Commission. They still thought He

---

99. Luke 18:31-34

100. Luke 24:19-21, emphasis added.

was going to raise an army and overthrow Rome. Right before His ascension, they asked Him, "Lord, will You at this time restore the kingdom to Israel?"[101]

This has a powerful impact on how we interpret scripture in the New Testament. When we read a passage about the "end of the age," we tend to think they are talking about the end of the world. But the Jews would have understood something completely different.

When people realized Jesus was the Messiah, He commanded them to keep it a secret. Why did He do this? Didn't He want people to know He was the Messiah? Once we understand the Jewish concept of the Messiah this makes sense.

Jesus knew that the Jews misunderstood His purpose. So, He reasoned that if they knew He was the Messiah, they would try to make Him king to overthrow Rome. And since this wasn't His mission, He tried to keep His identity hidden.

Jesus' concerns were well placed because some Jews did try to crown Him king. After Jesus had fed the five thousand, some Jews realized that He was the Messiah: "Therefore when Jesus perceived that they were about to come and take Him by force to make Him king, He departed again to the mountain by Himself alone" (John 6:15).

All of this tells us that the Jews did not see the "end of the age" as the end of the world. In fact, the end of

101. Acts 1:6

119

the world wasn't even part of the first century Jewish mindset. Their entire existence as the covenant people of God centered around the material world. The prophetic passages in the Old Testament, and the extra-biblical apocalyptic texts, told of a physical age of glory. The material world coming to an end was a Greek idea, not a Jewish one. N.T. Wright puts it well when he says:

> "The 'kingdom of god' has nothing to do with the world itself coming to an end. That makes no sense either of the basic Jewish worldview or of the texts in which the Jewish hope is expressed. It was after all the Stoics, not the first century Jews, who characteristically believed that the world would be dissolved in fire."[102]

And also here:

> "As good creational monotheists, mainline Jews were not hoping to escape from the present universe into some Platonic realm of eternal bliss enjoyed by disembodied souls after the end of the space-time universe. If they died in the fight for the restoration of Israel, they hoped not to 'go to heaven', or at least not permanently, but to be raised to new bodies when the kingdom came, since they would of course need new bodies to enjoy the very much this-worldly *shalom*, peace and prosperity that was in store."[103]

---

102. Wright, 285.

103. Wright, 286.

We cannot superimpose our modern Greek ideas of the end of the world onto the Jewish understanding of the "end of the age." As we will see, the destruction of Jerusalem in A.D. 70 fits all the prophetic passages that discuss the "end of the age." It just wasn't the one the Jews were expecting.

The Importance of the Temple

To better understand how the destruction of Jerusalem was the "end of the age," we have to understand the significance of the Temple within first century Judaism.

To the first century Jews, the Temple was the center of their world. Ancient Judaism was built upon sacrifice and offerings. Their relationship with God was dependent upon the sacrificial system (Leviticus 1-7). Without the sacrificial system, the Jews could not atone for their sins. In a real way, they were not God's people without the sacrificial system. Without it, they would not have been able to interact with God. The sacrificial system was the center of their covenant with God.

The Temple was also the dwelling place of God on the earth. This, for every practical reason, was the center of the Jewish world.

Furthermore, the Jews believed that they lived in the end times, and that "the end of the age" was right around the corner. Many Old Testament passages led first century Jews to believe that the end of the age would occur within their lifetimes. A pregnant expectation of "the end of the age" permeated the Jewish people in the first century. This ardent expectation was one of the reasons why Jews began to rebel more often during this period. As long as they endured and kept the covenant as best they could, they believed God would redeem His people.

Since they were expecting the restoration of Israel, the destruction of Jerusalem would have been a shocking fulfillment of the "end of the age." They thought they were on the verge of restoration, but instead God destroyed their city and leveled their Temple. With their Temple destroyed the sacrificial system ended. They could no longer atone for their sins. And they were cut off from the presence of God.

The sacrificial system established by Moses and practiced for over 1,500 years ended. Furthermore, it has never returned. Without it they were technically no longer Jews. Since the destruction of Jerusalem, the Jews have not been able to fulfill their part of their covenant. In a real way, Judaism was destroyed the day the Temple fell.

A branch of Judaism lives on to modern times, but it looks very different from first century Judaism. Without the Temple, they had to reinterpret what it meant to be Jewish.[104] Thus, the Judaism we find in the first century ceased to exist after A.D. 70, never to be reborn.

---

104. The "reinvention" of Judaism was more complicated than many imply, but over the course of next one hundred years, the Jews slowly began to piece together what it meant to be Jewish without access to the Temple, thereby fundamentally altering what it meant to be a Jew all the way up to the modern day.

In Matthew 24 (which we will study in a later chapter), the disciples asked Jesus when He would reveal Himself as the Messiah, restore Israel, and end the current age. This was it. The Jewish nation and God's covenant with the old Israel was destroyed. The New Israel was established in the Church. This New Israel would inherit the Kingdom and advance it throughout the entire world. This was the end of the age.

Instead of receiving their kingdom, the Jews lost it. This should not surprise us, for Jesus said it would happen:

"Have you never read in the Scriptures:

'The stone which the builders rejectedHas become
   the chief cornerstone.
 This was the Lord's doing,
 And it is marvelous in our eyes' ?

Therefore I say to you**, the kingdom of God will be taken from you and given to a nation bearing the fruits of it**. And whoever falls on this stone will be broken; but on whomever it falls, it will grind him to powder.'[105]

It may be difficult for modern Christians to understand the gravity of the destruction of Jerusalem. This was a massive shift in God's redemptive history. He wiped

---

105. Matthew 21:42-44, emphasis added.

away the Old Covenant, and firmly established the New.

We will discuss this in much greater detail when we study Revelation, but the "end of the age" was the end of God's covenant with Jerusalem. They rejected the Kingdom Jesus offered them, so He gave it to the New Israel, the Church.

The Book of Daniel Fulfilled

The Book of Daniel can't be about events in our future. It was supposed to be "unsealed" right before the events it predicted occurred. Not nearly 2,200 years later. The Book of Daniel was about the rise of Antiochus IV and then the destruction of Jerusalem. When the power of the Jews was "shattered."

The Book of Daniel is a powerful book that predicted the end of the Jewish age, but not the end of the world. The whole book builds to a world-changing event that would alter the course of history forever: Jesus' death and resurrection. This ushered in the Kingdom of God and started the process of global transformation.

Yet many still believe that these passages are about literal events in our future. The Pharisees were expecting the same thing when Jesus first came. They were so consumed by their understanding of the end times that they did not recognize the Messiah.

Could it be that the Church's fascination with the Antichrist has blinded her to the greatest move of God in history? We are in the midst of the greatest revival the world has ever seen. The gospel is spreading faster than it ever has before. Global poverty, hunger, and disease are all on the decline. There are more miracles happening today than in the first century. But since most of the Church is expecting an apocalypse, they can't see these things.

We need to check ourselves and make sure we are not making the same mistake as the Pharisees.

Part 3

MATTHEW 24

"When will these things take place?"

Chapter 1

WARS AND RUMORS OF WARS

"Truly, I say to you, this generation will not pass away until all these things take place." – Matthew 24:34, ESV

Matthew 24 (also known as the Olivet Discourse) is a major root for the apocalyptic understanding of the end times. According to many, Matthew 24 depicts a terrible period of reckoning right before the return of Jesus. But once we analyze the Olivet Discourse in reference to historical data, we will see it does not pertain to our future.

The Olivet Discourse is Jesus' response to a series of questions that the disciples ask Him. These questions will dictate how we understand Jesus' answer. We will see that the events recorded in the Olivet Discourse describe the fate of Jerusalem with great accuracy.

The Historical Context

Three gospels record The Olivet Discourse, but the Gospel of Matthew goes into greater detail than the other two. The Olivet Discourse occurred sometime between A.D. 27–A.D. 33. This 6-year window exists because scholars aren't exactly sure when Jesus was born. We also aren't sure where this passage falls within His ministry. But we can assume that it falls within this 6-year period.

Matthew, a disciple of Jesus, is the author of this account. Many also believe he was writing to a Jewish audience. Matthew attempts to root Jesus' teachings in Jewish culture. He also places a heavy emphasis on Jesus' fulfillment of Old Testament prophecies. He does so without explaining them to the reader. This implies that he assumed his readers were Jewish. These details in Matthew's account would have meant little to gentile converts.

This gives a different tone to Matthew 24. To understand what Jesus was trying to say, we need to know how first century Jews would have interpreted Him.

The Literary Context

Matthew 24 falls within a larger episode in scripture. In Matthew 23, Jesus prophesies judgment on the Pharisees and Jerusalem. He declares that God will soon judge them for all of Israel's sins in history.

Even though Matthew is broken into chapters and

verses, these distinctions are not part of the story. Scholars in the church added those later to help navigate scripture. Many times the chapter and verse markers do a good job of lining up with natural breaks in the story. But sometimes they placed chapter markers right in the middle of a narrative. Otherwise the chapter would have been hundreds of verses long, making it difficult to navigate. When this occurs, chapter markers can imply a break in the story that was not intended by the author.

Since there is no perceived gap in the narrative between Matthew 23 and 24, we must consider it one episode. This means that whatever occurred at the end of Matthew 23 impacts Matthew 24. If we do not study Matthew 23 first, it would be like opening a novel to chapter 20 and interpreting the story as if it began there. Thus, we must start our study of Matthew 24 with Matthew 23.

Matthew 23 contains the "Woe" episode in which Jesus condemns the Pharisees. He judges them for impeding the Kingdom (v. 13). Teaching new converts to do the same (v. 15). He judges them for their legalistic practices over access to God's presence (v. 16-22). He condemns them for following man-made religious regulations and abusing God's people to their own advantage (v. 23-24). And for hypocrisy (v. 25-28). In the end, He prophesies judgment over them because they would reject the Messiah and persecute the Church:

> "Therefore, indeed, I send you prophets, wise men, and scribes: some of them you will kill and crucify, and some

of them you will scourge in your synagogues and persecute from city to city, **that on you may come all the
righteous bloodshed on the earth**, from the blood of
righteous Abel to the blood of Zechariah, son of Bere-
chiah, whom you murdered between the temple and the
altar. **Assuredly, I say to you, all these things will come
upon this generation.**"[106]

Jesus states that God will judge the Pharisees for all of
Israel's sin. He says that this judgment will come within
"this generation."

"Generation" is the Greek word *genea*. It appears over
forty times in the New Testament. It refers to a group of
people born around the same time.

Some people have postulated that *genea* could mean
an undefined span of time. Maybe even thousands of
years. Their understanding of the end times forces them
to do this. Other passages in scripture (which we will get
to) uses the term "generation" in end times predictions.
Because they have a preconceived idea of how the end
will come, they have to find a way to interpret these
statements so they make sense. Since the world could
not have ended two thousand years ago, "generation"
can't mean a generation.

But, scripture never uses *genea* to mean an undetermined length of time. It is always in reference to a specific
group of people alive at a specific time.

The only way we can understand *genea* to mean

---

106. Matthew 23:34-36, emphasis added.

"thousands of years" is if we force our view of the end times onto it. Not only that, but the people to whom Jesus spoke would not have interpreted it this way.

The Book of Enoch shows us that first century authors would have clarified themselves if they meant thousands of years: "The angels showed me, and from them I heard everything, and from them I understood as I saw, *but not for this generation, but for a remote one which is to come.*" [107] Enoch was written between B.C. 300 to A.D. 100. It was a contemporary writing for the biblical authors. This means it sheds some light on how first century Jews would have understood things.

Enoch is not a canonical text. Meaning that most scholars do not believe God inspired it. But the Book of Jude references it. So the Biblical authors must have thought it was important.

The author of Enoch clarifies that his revelations were not meant for his generation. He says that they were for "a remote [generation] which is to come." This tells us that first century Jews understood the word "generation" to mean a generation. Not an undefined period of time. If they wanted to communicate an undefined period of time, they would have done so.

The Bible understands a generation to be forty years. For instance, God wanted one generation of Israelites to die before they entered the Promised Land. So He kept them in the wilderness for forty years.

---

107. The Book of Enoch 1:2

This means that Jesus' prophetic declarations to the Pharisees needed to have been fulfilled within 40 years. Jesus declared these judgments sometime around A.D. 30. Forty years later Rome destroyed Jerusalem in A.D. 70. Continuing in Matthew, just a few verses later, Jesus states that Jerusalem would be "left desolate" for her unfaithfulness:

"O Jerusalem, Jerusalem, the one who kills the prophets and stones those who are sent to her! How often I wanted to gather your children together, as a hen gathers her chicks under her wings, but you were not willing! See! **Your house is left to you desolate.**"[108]

This verse indicates that Jerusalem would be "left desolate" in judgment, which is exactly what happened in A.D. 70.

This scene sets the stage for Matthew 24. The narrative flows from chapter 23 to chapter 24. Right after Jesus' judgment, He and His disciples leave the Temple:

"Then Jesus went out and departed from the temple, and His disciples came up to show Him the buildings of the temple. And Jesus said to them, "Do you not see all these things? Assuredly, I say to you, not one stone shall be left here upon another, that shall not be thrown down."[109]

---

108. Matthew 23:37-39, emphasis added.

109. Matt. 24:1-2

Here is the scene. Jesus and His disciples were in the Temple when Jesus condemned the Pharisees. In that day, no one spoke to the Pharisees like Jesus did. They were the respected leaders of the community. To speak against them would be like speaking against the law and the prophets.

The disciples are silent during this encounter. They were probably shocked by what they were witnessing. Once Jesus finished, they turned to leave. You can imagine the deafening silence that rang throughout the Temple. The passage doesn't tell us this, but the disciples probably didn't know what to do with themselves.

As they were walking out, one could imagine that they tried to break the awkward silence (just like the Mount of Transfiguration[110]). They discussed architecture, pointing out the beautiful construction of the Temple (which they had seen many times before). Possibly an ancient equivalent to, "...What about them Yankees"?

But Jesus turns their attempt at small talk on its head. He tells them that the Temple would be destroyed.

The Temple stood at the center of the Jewish faith and covenant with God. Furthermore, the Jews believed the Messiah would be a warrior king who overthrew Rome and restored Israel. Thus, the destruction of the Temple would have confused the disciples. It ran contrary to their

---

110. On the Mount of Transfiguration, Peter, not knowing what to do with himself, suggested that they build three tabernacles for Jesus, Elijah, and Moses.

understanding of Israel's future. How could the Messiah overthrow Rome and restore Israel if the Temple was destroyed? In their confusion they asked Him to clarify:

> "Now as He sat on the Mount of Olives, the disciples came to Him privately, saying, 'Tell us, when will these things be? And what will be the sign of Your coming, and of the end of the age?"[111]

The disciples didn't understand what Jesus meant about the Temple. So they asked Him about it. Their questions set the stage for Matthew 24. The entire Olivet Discourse is Jesus' response to these questions. So, we must interpret His response through these questions. The disciples may not have understood His response. But Jesus' response would have related to their questions.

It is clear that the disciples asked Jesus three questions:

1) When will these things take place?

2) What will be the sign of your coming?

3) What will be the sign of the end of the age?

Their first question was, "when will *these things* take place?" To which things are they referring? What Jesus had just said: The destruction of Jerusalem and the Temple. When would God judge the Pharisees? When

---

111. Matthew 24:3

would He leave Jerusalem desolate? And when would the Temple be destroyed? They didn't understand how God could restore Israel if "these things" had to come to pass.

Their second question was, "what will be the sign of your coming?" The "sign of your coming" was an apocalyptic idiom pulled from Daniel 7 about the Messiah.

At this point within the narrative, the disciples knew Jesus was the Messiah (Matt. 16:16). But He told them not to tell anyone else (Mark 8:29-30). Thus, they were still expecting Him to reveal Himself as the Messiah to the Jewish people. They were asking, "When will you reveal yourself as the Messiah?"

The third question relates to their understanding of the Messiah. They ask, "What will be the sign of the end of the age?" The "end of the age" was not the same thing as the "end of the world." The coming of the Messiah and the restoration of Israel marked the "end of the age."

The Jews didn't even have a construct for the end of the world.[112] Since it wasn't in their minds, they wouldn't have asked about it. So, Jesus' response wasn't about the end of the world. It was about the destruction of the Temple and the end of the age.

For many Christians, a first century fulfillment of Matthew 24 doesn't seem possible. It is difficult to understand how the Great Tribulation could have occurred two thousand years ago. It also seems preposterous that Jesus' second coming occurred in A.D. 70.

---

112. Wright, 285.

Yet, once we take a closer look at Matthew 24 we will see that we have greatly misunderstood these passages. Jesus wasn't discussing His second coming. He didn't predict the Antichrist. Nor did He foretell the Great Tribulation (at least as most Christians understand it). Instead, Matthew 24 warns His disciples of the coming destruction of Jerusalem.

Our Temporal Anchor

How can one be so confident that Matthew 24 occurred within the first century? Because Jesus said it would. We are skipping ahead a little, but this frames our temporal understanding of the passage. Look at verse 34:

> "Assuredly, I say to you, this generation will by no means pass away till all these things take place."

Jesus states that everything He says would occur before the people to whom He was speaking died. He uses *genea* again. He is talking to a literal group of people. He was not speaking in metaphors. He was answering a very real question with a very real answer. They asked Him: "When will God judge Jerusalem and destroy the Temple?" He replied with: "Before this generation passes away." By Jesus' own mouth we must look for a first century fulfillment of this passage. And we have one.

In A.D. 70, Jerusalem was judged and the Temple was destroyed. Just as Jesus predicted.

Now that we have a grid to understand Matthew 24, let's go through it verse by verse to show how Jesus predicted these events.

Chapter 2

JESUS PREDICTS THE END

Jesus answers the disciples' questions starting in verse 4:

> "Take heed that no one deceives you. For many will come in My name, saying, 'I am the Christ,' and will deceive many."

The disciples ask, "When will these things take place?" Jesus says they will know it is close when self-proclaimed messiahs appear.

This verse is one reason why many Christians are looking for false christs to deceive the Church. They often use the presence of modern day heresies as proof that we are in the end times. But there were just as many heresies in Jesus' day, if not more.

The period just after Jesus' death and resurrection saw many false Messiahs. The Jews were desperate for a messiah to overturn Rome. Since Jesus did not look like the Messiah they expected, they looked to others to fit their expectations. Many surfaced proclaiming that they were the real Christ. In fact, many who had followed Jesus turned and followed these other false christs.

Justin Martyr sites examples of "false christs" attempting to deceive the people:

"After Christ's ascension into heaven the devils put forward certain men who said that they themselves were gods."[113]

Justin Martyr illustrates that a "number of men" claimed divine origin and led the people astray. Josephus (see chapter 1) also records that this period was ripe with "robbers and imposters who deluded the multitude."[114]

The forty years between Jesus' resurrection and the destruction of Jerusalem were turbulent times for the Jews. Many took advantage of this turbulence as means to their own end. One reason modern historians question the validity of the New Testament is that Jesus' claim to be a god-man Messiah wasn't unique.[115] This period was ripe with claims of part-man, part-god saviors. There were many copycats and false christs.

---

113. Justin Martyr, "The First Apology of Justin," *The Ante-Nicene Fathers, Vol 1,* (Buffalo, NY: Christian Literature Company, 1885), 171.

114. Josephus, *Antiquities* 20.160

115. Obviously Jesus' claim was unique. This is merely evidence that this period saw many false christs.

Matthew 24:6-7–Wars, Famines, and Earthquakes

Next, Jesus warns His disciples of coming wars, famines, and earthquakes:

> "And you will hear of wars and rumors of wars. See that you are not troubled; for all these things must come to pass, but the end is not yet. For nation will rise against nation, and kingdom against kingdom. And there will be famines, pestilences, and earthquakes in various places. All these are the beginning of sorrows."

This passage has led to many failed attempts to predict the end (much to the church's embarrassment). Many Christians claim that elevated violence in the modern world proves that we are in the last days. Yet, as we have already seen, we aren't in the most violent epoch in history. There were far worse periods in history. It just seems more violent today for reasons we have already discussed.

This passage fits the first century better. Jesus ministered at the tail end of the period known as the *Pax Romana* (the Roman Peace). This period marked a time of relative stability inside Rome's boarders, something Romans had not experienced in generations.[116]

This was especially true for Judea. With the coming of the Romans, wars in the region ended. Judea sat in the

---

116. Mary T. Boatwright and others, *The Romans: From Village to Empire* (New York, NY: Oxford University Press, 2004), 338.

crossroads to several powerful kingdoms. Egypt, Babylon, Assyria, the Greeks... Throughout history they all traveled through Judea to fight each other. For centuries Israel had armies marching through it. And sometimes those armies weren't nice to them. Now, because of Rome, trade could thrive. Communications were better than they had ever been. And there was a unified, though creaky, system of justice. [117]

But, the period after Jesus saw great violence across the empire. This disrupted the *Pax Romana*. Four emperors were assassinated. Many regions revolted (like Jerusalem). And foreign wars erupted. Many Roman historians thought Rome was on the brink of ruin. Going from the *Pax Romana* to this instability caused great worry within the empire. It also fueled the Jewish expectation that the Messiah would soon come.

There were also famines within this forty-year period. The New Testament itself even records this:

> "Agabus, stood up and showed by the Spirit that there was going to be a **great famine** throughout all the world, which also happened in the days of Claudius Caesar." [118]

This famine was so great that Paul made two pleas in the New Testament to help those suffering from it (Acts

---

117. Wright, 153-154.

118. Acts 11:28, emphasis added.

11:29-30, I Cor. 16:1-3). Eusebius, an early church historian, also gives an account of this great famine:

"Under him [Claudius] the world was visited with a famine, which writers that are entire strangers to our religion have recorded in their histories."[119]

There were also many earthquakes in this time period. Historians record that there were earthquakes in Colossae, Smyrna, Miletus, Chios, Samos, Laodicea, Heirapolis, Campania, Crete, Rome, and Judea including a 7.5 magnitude earthquake at Pompeii in A.D. 62.[120]

These wars, famines, and earthquakes fulfilled Jesus' prediction, and they answered the disciples questions. They were a warning that Jerusalem would soon be destroyed.

Matthew 24:9–Widespread Persecution

"Then they will deliver you up to tribulation and kill you, and you will be hated by all nations for My name's sake."

This verse leads many to believe that the Church will once again experience extreme persecution.

Christians around the world are experiencing great persecution today. Many see this as evidence that the end is near. But the number of countries persecuting the

---

119. Eusebius, *Histories*, 2.8.1.

120. Eberle, 26

Church is declining. None of the modern world powers persecute Christians.[121] Which was not true for the first century church.

The early Church experienced heavy persecution. The first persecution came from the Jews. Then, in A.D. 64, much of the city of Rome burned down. The emperor blamed Christians for it, thus beginning the first Roman persecution of the Church. These persecutions, both from the Jews and the Romans, were horrific. And considering the small size of the early church, they were massive. These events fit Jesus' warning in Matthew 24.

Matthew 24:10–The Great Apostasy

"And then many will be offended, will betray one another, and will hate one another."

This verse causes many Christians to look for a great apostasy (or falling away) in the modern Church. But there is a better first century fulfillment of this prediction.

This verse is a continuation of the previous verse. Jesus connects them by starting this verse with "And." He is saying there will be great persecutions (v. 9)... *and* people will fall way because of it (v. 10).

---

121. Some might consider China a world power and point out that they persecute the church. It is sad that China does this, but China is also experiencing one of the greatest revivals in history. Some estimate that 25,000 Chinese come to Christ every day. At this rate, China will soon become a Christian nation and the persecution will end.

The "great apostasy" was a first century event. During these persecutions, many early Christians turned their back on Christ. Some of them even reported other Christians to the authorities to save themselves, which is a direct fulfillment of this verse.

Matthew 24:11–False Prophets

"Then many false prophets will rise up and deceive many."

Jesus flows directly from persecution and apostasy to false prophets. We know that there were false prophets prior to the fall of Jerusalem. The New Testament authors recorded them:

"...many false prophets have gone out into the world"[122]

"False prophets also arose among the people, even as there will be false teachers among you, who will secretly introduce destructive heresies, even denying the Lord who bought them, and bring on themselves swift destruction"[123]

Here, both John and Peter discuss false prophets in the first century. These false prophets were both Gnostics and Judaizers – Jews who taught against Christ. We will discuss this more when we examine Revelation, but the Jews had a special relationship with Rome. Though tense,

---

122. 1 John 4:1

123. 2 Peter 2:1

Rome favored the Jews because they had an ancient religion (they respected anything ancient). And the Jews often turned to the Romans for support as they persecuted the early church. The Jews had no muscle under Roman rule, but they could convince the Romans to arrest or harass Christians (usually by false accusation). And many times the Romans simply turned a blind eye to Jewish "purges" of the Christian faith (think of the persecutions of Saul).

In the above verse, Peter states that these false prophets would experience "swift destruction." When the Jews rebelled against Rome, they lost their favor with Rome. And after Jerusalem was destroyed, the Judiazers vanished.

Matthew 24:12-13–Love Grows Cold

"And because lawlessness will abound, the love of many will grow cold. But he who endures to the end shall be saved."

Many believe this verse depicts a time of increased crime and violence in the world. But Jesus once again connects this statement to the previous verses with the word "and." It is in relation to the prior events that this occurs.

Josephus records that Judea experienced constant social degradation during the war with Rome. He states that as the Jews grew more desperate they robbed, killed, and even ate each other. He also states that there were survivors after the war, meaning that those who "endured to the end," and did not give up, were saved from death.[124]

---

124. Josephus, *Wars* 7.18

Matthew 24:14–The Global Gospel

"And this gospel of the kingdom will be preached in all the world as a witness to all the nations, and then the end will come."

Jesus says that the gospel must be preached throughout the entire world before the end will come. The gospel has advanced a great deal in modern times. This has caused many Christians to believe that we are in the last days. But there is a first century fulfillment of this verse supported by the New Testament itself.

Today, the "whole world" means every continent, nation, and people group on the planet. But the ancient world understood the "whole world" in a different way. They were not referring to the entire planet. They meant the entire civilized world. And at the time of the Roman Empire, they meant everything under Rome's control.

Nothing of important rested beyond the borders of Rome. They saw most people outside of the empire as uncivilized barbarians. Thus, there was nothing desirable beyond the borders of Rome. This mindset was so prevalent that Rome referred to the Mediterranean Sea as "Our Sea."

Furthermore, Paul thought of the "whole world" in these terms. He even believed that the gospel had been preached throughout the "whole world" within his lifetime:

"First, I thank my God through Jesus Christ for you all, that your faith is spoken of **throughout the whole world**."[125]

---

125. Romans 1:8, emphasis added.

"But I say, have they not heard? Yes indeed: 'Their sound [the gospel] has gone out to **all the earth, And their words to the ends of the world.**'"[126]

"Now to Him who is able to establish you according to my gospel and the preaching of Jesus Christ, according to the revelation of the mystery kept secret since the world began but now made manifest, and by the prophetic Scriptures **made known to all nations...**"[127]

"We give thanks to the God and Father of our Lord Jesus Christ, praying always for you, since we heard of your faith in Christ Jesus and of your love for all the saints; because of the hope which is laid up for you in heaven, of which you heard before in the word of the truth of the gospel, which has come to you, **as it has also in all the world**, and is bringing forth fruit..."[128]

"...if indeed you continue in the faith, grounded and stead-fast, and are not moved away from the hope of the gospel which you heard, **which was preached to every creature under heaven**, of which I, Paul, became a minister."[129]

Paul wrote these passages in the first century. Meaning there was a first century fulfillment of Matthew 24:14 for the early church.

Some might wonder if Paul and Jesus meant different things. Could Jesus have been referring to the whole

---

126. Romans 10:18, emphasis added.

127. Romans 16:25-26, emphasis added.

128. Colossians 1:5-6, emphasis added.

129. Colossians 1:23, emphasis added.

world, as we understand it today? While Paul was only talking about the civilized world? But a quick study of the Greek reveals that this is not the case.

There are several Greek words we translate as "world." There is *kosmos*, which translates as the "sum total of all created beings in heaven and earth; world, universe."[130] It's where we get our word "cosmos," meaning everything.

Paul uses *kosmos* twice in the verses mentioned above (Rom. 1:8; Col. 1:5-6). This means he thought that the gospel had spread throughout the whole cosmos by his time.

The other Greek word that we translate as "whole world" is *oikoumene*. But we shouldn't. We should translate it as the "inhabited part of the earth; world, inhabited earth."[131] It comes from the word *oikos*, which means "house." *Oikoumene* is the place where people live. This lines up with the ancient understanding of the "whole world" as well. Paul also uses *oikoumene* in Romans 10:18 mentioned above.

The surprising thing is that Jesus doesn't use *kosmos* in Matthew 24:14. He doesn't say that the gospel will spread throughout the "sum total of all created beings." He uses *oikoumene*. He says that the gospel must spread "throughout the civilized world."

Jesus stated that this would happen before "the end."

---

130. *Analytical Lexicon of the Greek New Testament*, 235.

131. *Analytical Lexicon of the Greek New Testament*, 279.

Remember that Jesus is answering a series of questions from the disciples about the end of the age. Not the end of the world. Jesus is saying that the gospel must spread throughout the civilized world before the end of the age. And the end of the age culminated in the destruction of Jerusalem in A.D. 70 (when the Temple was destroyed).

Rome executed Paul in A.D. 64, which was 6 years before Rome destroyed Jerusalem. This means Paul believed that the gospel had spread throughout the world before "the end of the age." This is a clear first century fulfillment of Matthew 24:14.

Eusebius believed this as well. He states:

> "The teaching of the new covenant was **borne to all nations**, and at once the Romans besieged Jerusalem and destroyed it and the Temple"[132]

John Chrysostom (an early church historian) said:

> "[It] is a very great sign of Christ's power, that in twenty or at most thirty years the **word had reached the ends of the world**. 'After this therefore,' saith He [Jesus], 'shall come the end of Jerusalem.'"[133]

---

132. Eusebius, *The Proof of the Gospel*, 1.6, trans. by W.J. Ferrar,, *Translations Of Christian Literature, Series I* (The Macmillan Company, New York, Ny: 1920). Emphasis added.

133. John Chrysostom, *Saint Chrysostom: Homilies on the Gospel of Saint Matthew*, vol. 10, A Select Library of the Nicene and Post-Nicene Fathers of the Christian Church, First Series (New York: Christian Literature Company, 1888), 452.

To the early church, the destruction of Jerusalem was the "sign of the final end." And the gospel had spread throughout the inhabited world before it happened, just as Jesus predicted.

Matthew 24:15-20–The Abomination of Desolation

"Therefore when you see the 'abomination of desolation,' spoken of by Daniel the prophet, standing in the holy place" (whoever reads, let him understand), let those who are in Judea flee to the mountains. Let him who is on the housetop not go down to take anything out of his house. And let him who is in the field not go back to get his clothes. But woe to those who are pregnant and to those who are nursing babies in those days! And pray that your flight may not be in winter or on the Sabbath"[134]

Many Christians use this passage to predict a coming Great Tribulation. They believe that the Jews will rebuild the Temple, and sometime after that the Antichrist will erect a statue of himself inside of it. Once this happens, global destruction will be close at hand.

But notice this passage does not mention the Antichrist. It references the Abomination of Desolation.

The abomination was first recorded in Daniel 7, which we have already discussed. It is clear that the "abomination" in Daniel was Antiochus IV.

---

134. Matthew 24:15-18

Antiochus' "reforms" in Jerusalem was one of the most traumatic periods in Israel's history. Nothing like it had ever happened to the Jews. Not only did Antiochus initiate brutal reforms, but he also ravaged Judea and left it desolate.

When a first century Jew heard the term "abomination of desolation spoken of by Daniel the prophet," they would have thought of Antiochus' and his reforms.

Then in A.D. 39 (roughly nine years after Jesus' warning), Emperor Caligula did something similar. He ordered that a statue of himself be constructed in the Jewish Temple. This action would have sparked memories of Antiochus IV in the Jewish mind. The Pharisees, attempting to avoid a deadly revolt, requested that Caligula reconsider. But instead Caligula told them that he would destroy Jerusalem and slaughter the Jews. Again, this would have brought flashbacks to Antiochus.

Caligula's military leaders advised him against it, but he didn't listen. Fortunately, Caligula died in A.D. 41, which averted the construction of the statue and the Jewish massacre.[135]

Even though the statue was never built, this threat served as a shocking reminder of Antiochus IV. Jesus was warning His disciples as to when "these things would take place." He told them, when you see something similar to the "reforms" of Antiochus IV coming, know that that the end of the age is near.

---

135. Josephus, *Antiquities*, 18:257-305.

Also, Jesus didn't mean that the abomination would come to the Temple specifically. But rather Jerusalem as a whole. The Greek word translated as "place" in this verse is *topos*, which is a geographical location. It denotes "a specific and defined area district, territory, land, or region."[136] It is not used to describe something as specific as a building or a room within a building. It is where we get our word "topography."

Furthermore, Luke describes the same event in a different way. He names Jerusalem as Matthew's "holy place":

> "**But when you see Jerusalem surrounded by armies, then know that its desolation is near**. Then let those who are in Judea flee to the mountains, let those who are in the midst of her depart, and let not those who are in the country enter her. For these are the days of vengeance, that all things which are written may be fulfilled. But woe to those who are pregnant and to those who are nursing babies in those days! For there will be great distress in the land and wrath upon this people. And they will fall by the edge of the sword, and be led away captive into all nations. And Jerusalem will be trampled by Gentiles until the times of the Gentiles are fulfilled."[137]

In both passages, Jesus advises people to "flee Judea" when they see the coming "desolation." In both passages,

---

136. *Analytical Lexicon of the Greek New Testament*, 382.

137. Luke 21:20-24, emphasis added.

Jesus grieves for the women who would be nursing during this time. And He prays that their flight would not be in the winter or on the Sabbath. The similarities between these passages, which are sometimes word-for-word, prove they are sister passages.

In Luke's version, Jesus doesn't say "the holy place," but rather "Jerusalem." Remember, Matthew was writing to the Jews, who would have understood the term "holy place" to refer to Jerusalem. But Luke was writing to gentile readers who would not have understood that term. So he clarified the point by naming Jerusalem.

Furthermore, when Luke discusses the "abomination" he speaks of an army encamped around Jerusalem. To the Jews, who were expecting the Messiah to overthrow Rome, the Roman army (gentiles) sieging Jerusalem would have been an abomination.

When Jesus referred to the "abomination," He was comparing what happened to the Jews under Antiochus to what would happen to them under Rome.

Furthermore, a global event doesn't fit the description in either passage. Luke's version of the events makes it clear that Jesus is talking about the destruction of Jerusalem. Not the whole world.

Secondly, Jesus' warning is geo-specific to Judea and ethno-specific to the Jews. He prays that their flight wouldn't be in the winter. It isn't winter all over the world at the same time, so He can't be talking about the whole world. He also prays that their flight isn't on the Sabbath. Only the Jews recognize the Sabbath.

Thirdly, Jesus states, "let those who are in Judea" flee from Jerusalem. If this were a global tribulation, why would only those in Judea need to flee? And why would fleeing to the hills help if this were a global event? A localized event in Judea and Jerusalem makes much more sense.

Finally, John Chrysostom corroborates this by recording:

> "Having spoken of the ills that were to overtake the city [Jerusalem]… He mentions again the Jews' calamities… 'Then,' saith He, 'let them which be in Judea flee into the mountains.' Then, When? When these things should be, 'when the abomination of desolation should stand in the holy place.' **Whence be seems to me to be speaking of the armies**."[138]

This was a warning to Christians in Jerusalem. Luke makes it very clear:

> "But when you see **Jerusalem surrounded by armies**, then know that its desolation is near. **Then let those who are in Judea flee to the mountains**, let those who are in the midst of her depart, and let not those who are in the country enter her."[139]

One of the shocking things about this passage is that Eusebius recorded that early Christians took this warning to heart

---

138. John Chrysostom, *Homilies on the Gospel of Saint Matthew*, Homily LXXVI. Emphasis added.

139. Luke 21:20-21, emphasis added.

and fled when they heard that the Romans were coming:

> "But the people of the church in Jerusalem had been commanded by a revelation [Matt. 24], vouchsafed to approved men there before the war, to leave the city and to dwell in a certain town of Perea called Pella. And when those that believed in Christ had come thither from Jerusalem, then, as if the royal city of the Jews and the whole land of Judea were entirely destitute of holy men, the judgment of God at length overtook those who had committed such outrages against Christ and his apostles, and totally destroyed that generation of impious men."[140]

These Christians were spared from the coming judgment because of Jesus' warning in Matthew 24. Jesus' prophetic warning saved many early Christians from the horrors of the siege that would follow. This passage was not only fulfilled in the first century, but it saved thousands of lives as well.

Matthew 24:21-22–The Great Tribulation

> "For then there will be great tribulation, such as has not been since the beginning of the world until this time, no, nor ever shall be. And unless those days were shortened, no flesh would be saved; but for the elect's sake those days will be shortened."

---

140. Eusebius, *Church History, Life of Constantine the Great, and Oration in Praise of Constantine*, ed. Philip Schaff and Henry Wace, trans. Arthur Cushman McGiffert, 3.5.3. *The Nicene and Post-Nicene Fathers of the Christian Church*, Second Series, vol. 1 (New York: Christian Literature Company, 1890), 138.

This passage is where we get the term "Great Tribulation." The "Great Tribulation" is also associated with events recorded in Daniel and Revelation. But to better understand this passage, we must look at its sister passage in Luke:

> "For there will be great distress in the land and wrath **upon this people**. And they will fall by the edge of the sword, and be **led away captive into all nations**. And **Jerusalem will be trampled by the Gentiles...**"[141]

Luke brings some clarity to this passage. He states that the Great Tribulation is specific to Jerusalem. He says that judgment and wrath will fall "upon this people." Not "all people." He says that they will "fall by the edge of the sword" and that they will be "led away captive into all nations." If this is talking about the whole world, how can a specific people be hauled away? Finally, Luke names Jerusalem as the recipient of judgment.

Jesus also stated the Great Tribulation would stop so that not everyone would perish.

We will discuss the horrors of the siege of Jerusalem in more depth later, but the inhabitants suffered great horrors. Famine, plague, and death reigned in the city. When the Roman soldiers finally entered, they found houses full of the bodies of people who had died from starvation or disease. There were eight thousand bodies in the Temple alone. If the Romans had continued the

---

141. Luke 21:23-24a, emphasis added.

siege instead of taking the city by force, everyone inside would have died. But, just as Jesus predicted, the siege ended and there were survivors.

When people first hear this, they may think: "How can the worst tribulation in human history have had already occurred? Jesus said it would be worse than any tragedy in history. How could the destruction of Jerusalem meet that criterion? Wasn't the Holocaust worse? What about all the other terrible things that have occurred in the world?" This is a great question, and to answer it we need to understand how the ancient world would have understood it.

Josephus, who saw Jerusalem's destruction, used similar language to describe it. He said that it was the most terrible event he could have ever imagined. He said that the Jews were reduced to cannibalism (parents ate their young). He said that disease ran rampant throughout the city. And he claimed that the Roman slaughter caused the streets to literally run with blood. When Rome finally conquered Jerusalem, they burned the Temple and tore it down. Then, all the survivors were forced out of Jerusalem and sent all over the empire. Which Jesus predicted in Luke's version. This is what Josephus has to say about it:

> "... It had so come to pass, that our city Jerusalem had arrived at a higher degree of felicity than any other city under the Roman government, and yet at last fell into the sorest of calamities again. **Accordingly it appears to me, that the misfortunes of all men, from the beginning**

of the world, if they be compared to these of the Jews, are not so considerable as they were."[142]

Was the destruction of Jerusalem really the worst event in human history? We cannot know for certain. Was Jesus speaking in hyperbole? It is possible. Yet, it is interesting that the authoritative historian on the destruction of Jerusalem used the same words as Jesus did to predict it.

Matthew 24:23-26–False Signs and Wonders

"Then if anyone says to you, 'Look, here is the Christ!' or 'There!' do not believe it. For false christs and false prophets will rise and show great signs and wonders to deceive, if possible, even the elect. See, I have told you beforehand. Therefore if they say to you, 'Look, He is in the desert!' do not go out; or 'Look, He is in the inner rooms!' do not believe it."

In this passage, Jesus states that many false christs and prophets would arise in attempt to deceive the people. As we've already discussed, history records that this period was ripe with messiahs and demi-gods. Josephus corroborates this. He says that there were false prophets immediately before the destruction of Jerusalem. Here's one example:

"And now these impostors and deceivers persuaded the multitude to follow them **into the wilderness,** and

---

142. Josephus, *Wars,* 1:11-12, emphasis added.

pretended that they would **exhibit manifest wonders and signs,** that should be performed by the providence of God... Moreover, there came out of Egypt about this time to Jerusalem, one that said **he was a prophet**, and advised the multitude of the common people to go along with him to the Mount of Olives...He said farther, that he would show them from hence, how, at his command, the walls of Jerusalem would fall down..."[143]

Josephus records that many "imposters and deceivers" caused people to "follow them into the wilderness," which should remind us of Jesus' warning: "Therefore if they say to you, 'Look, He is in the desert!' do not go out."

Josephus goes on to state that the Romans "subdued" (i.e. killed) most of the people following these false prophets. To Rome, claims of messiahship were dangerous. They could rile up the people into fervor. So they took aggressive actions as more of them appeared.

Jesus' warning kept the disciples safe from the Roman executions. He was saying, "If you hear claims that I have returned, and that I am out in the desert, don't believe them. They are lying to you, and if you follow them you will be killed."

---

143. Josephus, *Antiquities*, 20.167-170, emphasis added.

Matthew 24:29–The Stars Will Fall From Heaven

"Immediately after the tribulation of those days the sun will be darkened, and the moon will not give its light; the stars will fall from heaven, and the powers of the heavens will be shaken."

Many understand Matthew 24:27-31 to be about Jesus' second coming. In fact, many Bibles even place a subhead here that say, "The Second Coming." But Jesus wasn't talking about the second coming. He was continuing His prediction of the end of the age.

For us to understand these verses, we need to understand Jewish apocalyptic language and idioms. Matthew wrote his Gospel for the Jews. So he would have used imagery and language familiar to Jews. Language that may be difficult for us to understand today.

Throughout the Old Testament, the sun, moon, and stars symbolized authority. For example, Joseph had a dream about the sun, moon, and stars bowing down to him. His parents did not interpret this to mean the heavens would bow down to him. Instead, they knew it was about them. Which offended them.

Also, in Revelation 12:1, there is a woman described as having the moon and sun under her feet and stars crowned upon her head. We know this is not talking about a literal woman who stood on the moon and sun and wore stars as a hat. It represents a woman of great power.

We have similar phrases today when we say that

someone is "stellar" or a "superstar." We don't mean that they are giant balls of fusing hydrogen. We mean they shine with fame and glory. This is how the Jews used these symbols as well. They represented glory and power. And quite often they were symbolic for kings, kingdoms, or other powerful entities.

Thus, when these heavenly bodies were "darkened" or "fell from heaven," it was an idiom for their judgment. We have similar language when we say that someone "fell from grace." We mean that they lost their fame and influence.

To illustrate this in the Bible, look at these Old Testament passages. The first one is a judgment of Egypt (this passage is not talking about the events recorded in Exodus, but a later judgment of Egypt):

> "When I put out your light, I will cover the heavens, and **make its stars dark**; I will **cover the sun** with a cloud, And **the moon shall not give her light**. All the bright lights of the heavens **I will make dark over you**, And bring darkness upon your land,' says the Lord God."[144]

God judged Egypt, but there isn't a record of the sun darkening or the disappearance of the stars. God used imagery of the sun, moon, and stars going dark to describe Egypt's fall from grace.

Next, look at this judgment of Edom in Isaiah:

---

144. Ezekiel 32:7-9, emphasis added.

"**All the host of heaven shall be dissolved,** And the heavens shall be rolled up like a scroll; **All their host shall fall down** As the leaf falls from the vine, And as fruit falling from a fig tree. For My sword shall be bathed in heaven; Indeed it shall come down on Edom, And on the people of My curse, for judgment."[145]

Again, Edom (the northern parts of ancient Israel) was judged and destroyed. But the sun, moon, and stars did not literally go dark. Nor did they fall from the sky. Edom's power and authority was taken from her when Assyria destroyed her.

As another example, look at God's judgment of Babylon:

"For the stars of heaven and their constellations Will not give their light; The sun will be darkened in its going forth, And the moon will not cause its light to shine."[146]

Babylon was judged, but the sun, moon, and stars did not darken.

These passages reveal that Jewish culture used these images to refer to judgment and destruction. Which fits Jerusalem's judgment in the first century. Jesus was saying that Jerusalem's place in the world as a covenantal people was coming to an end.

---

145. Isaiah 34:4-5, emphasis added.

146. Isaiah 13:10

Matthew 24:30a–The Sign of the Son of Man

"Then the sign of the Son of Man will appear in heaven..."

Many will assert that this verse refers to Jesus' second coming. Yet, if we look close at it, Jesus doesn't say that the Son of Man would appear. He says the *sign* of the Son of Man would appear in "heaven." That is different.

Many translations render this verse as saying that the sign would appear in the sky. But that isn't what the Greek says. The Greek word for "sky" is *ourano*, which means "heaven." You can translate it as "heaven" or "the heavens," meaning the vast array of stars in the sky. But the Jews would have understood this to be symbolic language representing kingdoms and powers.

Furthermore, remember that the disciples asked Him "what will be the sign of your coming?" meaning "when will you reveal yourself as the Messiah?" His response is: "The destruction of Jerusalem will be my sign. I will announce to the world that I am the Messiah when you see Jerusalem fall from grace and her authority taken from her. This will be my public announcement that the previous age has ended and a new age has begun."

Early church fathers understood that the destruction of Jerusalem proved the Jesus was the Messiah. Tertullian said this:

"So likewise that conditional threat of the sword, 'If ye refuse and hear me not, the sword shall devour you,' has proved that it was Christ, for rebellion against whom [the Jews] have perished."[147]

Tertullian, in fighting a gnostic heresy, states that the destruction of Jerusalem proved Jesus was the Messiah.

When God destroyed Jerusalem, it stood as a sign of her judgment for adultery. And it revealed that the Old Covenant had been wiped away.

Idolatry is the spiritual version of adultery. In the natural we commit adultery when we break our covenant with a spouse. When you worship other gods, you are committing spiritual adultery on God.

The Old Testament punishment for adultery is death. Also, God had an Old Testament precedent for punishing His people for idolatry with an invading army.[148]

In A.D. 70, Rome destroyed Jerusalem and ancient Judaism ceased to exist. The disciples asked Him when He would reveal Himself as the Messiah and end the current age. This was it. The destruction of Jerusalem was the end of the age.

---

147. Tertullian, "The Five Books Against Marcion," in *Latin Christianity: Its Founder, Tertullian*, ed. Alexander Roberts, James Donaldson, and A. Cleveland Coxe, trans. Peter Holmes, vol. 3, The Ante-Nicene Fathers (Buffalo, NY: Christian Literature Company, 1885), 341.

148. God punished Edom with the Assyrian Army and Jerusalem with the Babylonian Army.

Matthew 24:30b–All The Tribes Will Mourn

"... and then all the tribes of the earth will mourn,..."

To better understand this verse, we need to better understand the Greek word for "earth."

The Greek word used here for "earth" is *he ge*, which can we can translate as either "the earth" or "the land."[149] Our translations tend to render this word as "earth." But it is more likely that first century Jews would have understood it to mean "land."

First century Jews used a Greek translation of the Old Testament called the Septuagint. In this translation, the Promised Land of God was referred to as "the land," or *he ge*. Thus, to first century Jews, *he ge* would have meant "the Promised Land," or "Judea." It would not have meant the whole world.

This has a dramatic impact on the meaning of this verse. It means that Jesus said that all the tribes of *the land* would mourn, which happened. All the tribes of *the land* (i.e., the Jews, the twelve tribes) mourned the destruction of Jerusalem. Their holy city and their Temple had been destroyed.

---

149. *Analytical Lexicon of the Greek New Testament*, 98.

Matthew 24:30c–Jesus Returns In The Roman Army

> "... and they will see the Son of Man coming on the clouds
> of heaven with power and great glory."

Notice that Jesus did not say that the Son of Man would
return to the earth, but in heaven (Gk. *ourano*) And that
the Son of Man will be clothed in power and great glory.
This is exactly what happened.

After Jesus died and rose again, He was seated in power
at the right hand of the Father. The destruction of Jerusalem was the proof of His Messiahship (and Jerusalem's
error). It also demonstrated the end of the age predicted
in the Old Testament.

We must understand that God often "came to people"
in judgment through an army. He did not materialize.
Throughout the Old Testament He used other nations
to carry out His judgments.[150] In this same way, Jesus
returned to Jerusalem in the form of the Roman army.

Josephus also offers a fascinating support for this
interpretation. During the siege, the Romans constructed
catapults to hurl large stones at Jerusalem. When the
Romans launched their rocks, Josephus recorded that the
Jews would warn those on the walls by saying:

> "...Accordingly the watchmen that sat upon the towers
> gave them notice when the engine was let go, and the

---

150. See Malachi 4:6 NIV, Hosea 10:11 NASB.

THE END OF DAYS

stone came from it, and cried out aloud in their own country language, "THE SON COMES:"[151]

It appears that the Jews were declaring their own judgment without realizing it. It is unlikely they knew what they were saying. It's not clear if Josephus knew what they meant either. It seems as though he included this detail because of its oddness. If God can cause a donkey to talk, He can certainly make people prophesy their own judgment without their knowledge.[152]

---

151. Josephus,*Wars*, 5.272

152. There is a debate about the Greek in this passage. Some believe there was an error in the manuscripts. But there is considerable evidence that this isn't so.

First off, Josephus wrote this history in two editions, one in the language of the Chaldeans, and another in Greek. In both, Josephus writes "The Son Comes," which should settle the debate.

Yet, others have argued there is an error in the Greek. They say that Josephus misspelled the word for "son." They argue that the Greek word for "son," *huios*, could have been confused with the Greek word for "arrow" or "dart," *ios*. But the Romans were not throwing darts or arrows. They were throwing large stones. If Josephus were trying to say "The Stone Comes," he would have used *petros*, which is not close to *huios*. And there would have been no reason to include this in histories since there is nothing unique about it.

Furthermore, *ios* is a poetic form of the "arrow" or "dart." People did not use it in prose (Josephus only wrote in prose). All this means that Josephus meant to record "The Son Comes."

Matthew 24:31–The Angels Gather The Elect

"And He will send His angels with a great sound of a
trumpet, and they will gather together His elect from the
four winds, from one end of heaven to the other."

Many think that this verse is about the rapture. But only
three verses later Jesus states that "this generation will by
no means pass away until all of these things take place."
He anchors these events within the first century.

When Jesus sat down at the right hand of the Father, He
had all authority on Heaven and earth (Matthew 28:18).
Blowing a trumpet in the ancient world represented a
royal decree. This decree released angels to go gather His
people from all over the world. This doesn't mean the
angels removed Christians from the earth. It means that
God's people would now come from all people groups.

Before Jesus came, only the Jews had access to God.
After Jesus' ministry, the gospel opened to all peoples.
Jesus sent His disciples to preach the gospel to Jews
and the gentiles. At the same time, He released angelic
powers to reinforce their mission. They were plucking
people out of Satan's deception and placing them within
Christ's kingdom.

Furthermore, many Christians lived in Jerusalem
during its birth. But the destruction of Jerusalem forced
them out into the rest of the world. And history illustrates
that Christianity began its explosive growth after the
destruction of Jerusalem.[153]

---

153. Eberle, 62.

THE END OF DAYS

Matthew 24:37–As In The Days of Noah

"But as the days of Noah were, so also will the coming of the Son of Man be."

This verse causes many to believe that the world will get worse right before the end. They believe the world will slip into a state of moral decay only paralleled by the period immediately before the flood of Noah. Therefore, according to this interpretation, we must look for the world to get worse before Jesus will return.

First off, He is not discussing His second coming. There is no perceived gap between the previous verses. The "coming of the Son of Man" is a reference to the end of the age, not the end of the world.

Additionally, this passage is not discussing the moral state of Judea before Jesus' "return." But rather the suddenness of His judgment. If we take a closer look at the verse in context, this will become clear:

"But of that day and hour no one knows, not even the angels of heaven, but My Father only. But as the days of Noah were, so also will the coming of the Son of Man be. For as in the days before the flood, they were eating and drinking, marrying and giving in marriage, until the day that Noah entered the ark, and did not know until the flood came and took them all away, so also will the coming of the Son of Man be."[154]

154. Matthew 24: 36-39

172

This passage is not discussing the morality of Noah's time, but rather the timing of the flood. Jesus says that in the days of Noah people did not believe the flood was coming. So they lived their lives as normal–right up until the flood hit. Jesus is drawing a parallel to Jerusalem's destruction. The Jews won't know that their judgment is coming until it is right upon them. Which is what happened.

Up until the final hour, the Jews believed God would save them and vindicate them in front of the gentiles. Thus, their destruction came as a complete surprise.

Concluding Thoughts on Matthew 24

This analysis of Matthew 24 reveals that Jesus was discussing the destruction of Jerusalem in A.D. 70. It had nothing to do with the end of the world. His disciples asked Him a series of questions about the Temple, when He would reveal Himself as the Messiah to the world, and when the age would end. He answered their questions, giving His disciples a clear timetable of events. And He gave them warnings, which the early church followed. Matthew 24 was a thoughtful response to the concerns of His disciples. It reveals a shepherd looking after His flock, and a warning for the coming storm.

Part 4

THE BOOK OF REVELATION

"The Revelation of Jesus Christ, which God gave Him
to show His servants—things which must shortly take
place... Blessed is he who reads and those who hear the
words of this prophecy, and keep those things which are
written in it; for the time is near." – Rev. 1:1, 3

We have now come to the biggest enigma in the Bible.
The Book of Revelation is one of the most confusing
books for modern readers. Many Christians have given
up hope in ever understanding it. They even avoid it.
This is unfortunate, because Jesus promises that those
who read it will receive a blessing.

Revelation doesn't have to confuse us. When we
approach it from a first century perspective, there is a
lot to glean from it. Though its imagery may seem foreign and confusing, Revelation can be one of the most
inspiring and beautiful books in the Bible.

Chapter 1

THE APOCALYPSE OF JOHN

The Book of Revelation's real name is The Apocalypse of John. Apocalypse means an "uncovering, disclosing, or revealing."[155] In scripture, this is often the revealed knowledge of God. Apocalypse does not mean "the destruction of the world."

We call it the Book of Revelation because it contains a revelation John received from God. We use "apocalypse" to mean "the end of the world" because that is what many people believe Revelation depicts. But it is not. There are just too many similarities between the destruction of Jerusalem and the Book of Revelation to ignore.

Revelation has been the fodder for more misinformation than possibly any other text in existence. Its grand and often bizarre images have inspired countless attempts at interpretation. And these interpretations have left people more confused and afraid than enlightened.

---

155. *Analytical Lexicon of the Greek New Testament*, 67.

Yet, God does not motivate with fear, so we should discard any interpretation that promotes fear. Revelation should leave you with a firm comfort in the sovereignty of God. And it should give you a bright hope for the future of the Church.

Revelation is not about a future battle of Armageddon or even Jesus' second coming. Revelation predicted the destruction of Jerusalem in A.D. 70. It described the church's vindication against Judaism. And it illustrates God's plan for His church today.

"The Time Is Near"

In the first few verses of Revelation we learn that it is about events "which must shortly come to pass" (Rev.1:1).

Many Christians have come to interpret "shortly" (or "soon" in other translations) to mean "thousands of years." We have interpreted it this way because we have forced our eschatology onto the text. Since we assume that the book is about the end of the world, we have to reinterpret these verses to fit our ideas. But there is no need to do this. Once we entertain the idea that Revelation is about the destruction of Jerusalem, "soon" can mean soon.

Some Christians defend this reinterpretation of "soon" with 2 Peter 3:8. Here, Peter states that to God one day is like a thousand years and a thousand years are like one day. This is evidence for many Christians that God's definition of soon can be different than our own. But 2 Peter 2:8 is a passing verse on a different subject.

Peter is comforting a group of Christians that were afraid they had missed Jesus' return. He tells them that Jesus is not being "slack" in His promises since He hadn't yet returned. Revelation is not about Jesus' return or the end of the world. It is about God's establishment of a new people and the wiping away the old covenant.

Revelation is a warning to the early church. It predicted turbulent times as Rome destroyed Jerusalem and persecuted the church. But it comforts the church by giving Christians a vision of what is to come. It gives the early church context for their trials and reassures her that God has great plans for her.

Also, this long interpretation of "soon" would have meant nothing to the original audience. And there is no evidence for this interpretation within Revelation itself. Jesus was talking to seven literal churches about real hardships they were experiencing. Therefore, it does not make sense that Jesus would use a timetable that meant nothing to the original audience. His promises of protection and provision would have been merciless taunts if they had been intended for time and people in their distant future.

There are some Christians who believe that the Seven Letters were not meant for real churches. Instead they were predictions about seven "dispensations" of church history.[156] And since the seventh church was backslidden, they expect the last days to be turbulent times. But

156. Gentry and others, *Four Views on the Book of Revelation*, 42.

that idea is a much later construction and interpretation of Revelation.

The Seven Letters go to seven cities that fall on an ancient mail route through Asia Minor. This leads many scholars to believe that the Seven Letters went to seven real churches. Also, the "dispensation" idea doesn't take the literary style or the historical context into consideration (we will discuss this in greater depth later).

Furthermore, the Greek leaves little room for the "long – soon" interpretation. The Greek word that John uses for "soon" is *tachos*. It means with "speed, haste, and swiftness." And as an adverb, it means "without delay, at once, speedily."[157] Nowhere in the Bible is this word used to mean "an undetermined span of time." It is always meant to communicate "very quickly."

For instance, in the Book of Acts, the Lord warns Paul to move "hastily" to avoid imprisonment: "Make haste and get out of Jerusalem *quickly*, for they will not receive your testimony concerning Me." [158] Here the word for "quickly" is *tachos,* and it clearly means "quickly."

There are some who argue that Jesus used the word "soon" in Revelation so that we will live with constant vigilance and motivation. This implies that we need the slave master of fear at our backs for us to do our work. If Jesus used "soon" in this way, it means that Jesus lied

---

157. *Analytical Lexicon of the Greek New Testament*, 376.

158. Acts 22:18.

to His children in the first century to manipulate them into action. This is not Jesus.

This view also takes a low view of humanity. It claims that fear over His return should be our motivation rather than an expression of our love for Him.

Some also believe that the Book of Revelation could have a duel fulfillment. Meaning that it could be discussing events in the first century, as well as events in our future. But, again, there isn't any scriptural evidence for this. As with Matthew 24, we have to read that into the text to arrive at this conclusion. If Nero fulfilled all the prophecies about the "Beast" in Revelation, why look for any other fulfillment? What does Jesus say that implies we need to look for multiple fulfillments?

Also, the book ends with an angel warning John not to "seal the words of the prophecy of this book, for the time is at hand" (Rev. 22:20). This should remind us of Daniel's instruction. Daniel was told to "seal up" his prophecies until right before the end. The prophecies that were given to Daniel were of the distant future. So, God told Daniel to seal them until right before their fulfillment. But John's command stands in direct contrast by saying, "don't seal these words, for the time is now." This correlation is not by accident. It is a strategic use of Jewish idioms to get the attention of early Christians, and God uses these idioms to communicate that these events are about to occur.

The book is wrapped by the imperative suddenness of these events. This leaves little room for progressive or dual fulfillment interpretations. The book makes it clear to the original audience that these events would occur in their near future.

The Date

The Book of Revelation is a prophetic book. Jesus states that Revelation predicts events that had not yet occurred when John wrote it (Rev. 1:19). This plays a big role in how we interpret Revelation. If John wrote it after the fall of Jerusalem, then it can't be about Jerusalem's fate. It would have to be about later events. Possibly even events in our future.

Many scholars believe that John wrote Revelation around A.D. 95. Others believe he wrote it between A.D. 64-68. Since Jerusalem fell in A.D. 70, this debate plays a critical role in interpreting Revelation. So, lets examine the evidence for each theory.

John states that Jesus gave him his vision while he was on Patmos (Rev. 1:9). Emperor Domitian exiled John to Patmos between A.D. 81-96.[159] This has caused many to believe that John wrote Revelation around A.D. 95.

Yet, there is evidence that John was exiled to Patmos several times. Early Church historian Epiphanius

---

159. Irenaeus of Lyons, "Irenæus Against Heresies," in *The Apostolic Fathers with Justin Martyr and Irenaeus*, 5.30.3 ed. Alexander Roberts, James Donaldson, and A. Cleveland Coxe, vol. 1, The Ante-Nicene Fathers (Buffalo, NY: Christian Literature Company, 1885), 559–560.

stated that Claudius Caesar exiled John to Patmos as well. Claudius died in A.D. 54. But older manuscripts and inscriptions referred to Nero as "Claudius Nero" or "Claudius Nero Caesar." Because of this, some scholars believe that Epiphanius meant Nero, not Claudius.[160] Either way, it suggests that John was also at Patmos before the fall of Jerusalem.

Furthermore, the Syriac, one of the oldest versions of the New Testament, states that John wrote Revelation when Nero exiled him to Patmos.[161] Nero was emperor from A.D. 54-68. This is just a few years before the fall of Jerusalem.

Finally, Revelation predicts the imminent fulfillment of its prophecies. If John recorded Revelation in A.D. 95, then we must ignore its urgency. But the Book's imminent warnings fit with the earlier date of authorship. If John composed Revelation when Nero exiled him, it would put Revelation just a few years before Jerusalem's fall. His warnings would have been real. They would have been relevant. And they would have had meaning for the original and intended audience.

Therefore, with all of this evidence taken together, it is logical to assume that John wrote Revelation before the destruction of Jerusalem.

---

160. Edwards Ellis, *The Making of the New Testament Documents* (Leiden, Netherlands, 1999), 214.

161. Ellis, 214.

A Global Event

Many people believe that Revelation is about a global event. This is because Revelation uses language like the "whole world" when discussing judgment and destruction. With this lens, it is hard to see how Revelation could be about the destruction of Jerusalem.

But this is another point where our eschatology has influenced our translations. The Greek word used throughout Revelation for "the world" is *he ge*. As we already saw in Matthew 24, *he ge* means the earth. It is the ground, the dirt, and substance beneath our feet. In English, "the earth" can mean "the ground" or "the planet." In the same way, *he ge* can mean "the world" or "the land." And there is reason to believe the Jews and Christians would have read it as "the land."

In the first century, Jews and Christians used a Greek translation of the Old Testament called the Septuagint (also known as the LXX). The LXX used *he ge* to refer to the Promised Land (or "the Land"). This means that first century Judeo-Christians would not have understood *he ge* to mean the world. When Revelation discussed *he ge*, they would have read "the land," meaning Judea.

This changes how we read Revelation. It reveals that Revelation isn't about a global event, but rather a local one. Instead of judgment falling on the world, it often says that judgment will fall on *the land*. Or more precisely, the Promised Land (Judea). And this is exactly what happened.

Apocalyptic Language

The apocalyptic language John used to write Revelation can confuse modern Christians as well.

By the first century, apocalyptic literature saturated the Jewish world. Apocalyptic authors used Old Testament prophetic images to convey their messages. Apocalyptic writings were associated with ecstatic, spiritual experiences. Some authors claimed God inspired them. But not all. Instead, they used imagery from their own prophetic history to write about their current situation. They also used it to illustrate how past events affected their present reality.

We do this in present day as well. For instance, one might describe the fall of the Berlin Wall as an "earth-shattering event." Yet, we do not mean that an earthquake shook and brought down the wall. The same is true of apocalyptic imagery.

Apocalyptic writings also used "complex and highly colored metaphors in order to describe one event in terms of another, thus bringing out the perceived 'meaning' of the first."[162] This was a "reinvestment" of one image into another. According to N.T. Wright (a New Testament theologian we have referenced earlier in this book), this "reinvestment" helps readers better understand the event in question.

John uses this tactic throughout Revelation. The seals,

---

162. Wright, 282.

trumpets, and bowls are all reinvestments of the judgment of Jerusalem. They paint a vibrant picture of God's judgment of the Jews.

John also sees the same event from different perspectives. For instance, the bowls of wrath and the fall of Babylon are discussing the same event. Many interpret these as two separate episodes. But John reinvests the destruction of the great prostitute into the bowls of wrath. This intensifies the imagery and gives us more detail.

The futurist commentator Robert Mounce even recognizes this: "That the language of prophecy is highly figurative has nothing to do with the reality of the events predicted. Symbolism is not a denial of historicity but a matter of literary genre."[163] The question is not whether John was speaking in symbolic language. He was. The question is what he meant by that language.

Moreover, Christians used apocalyptic literature as a "code" to avoid Roman authorities. Since Christians did not worship the Roman gods, Romans often blamed Christians for famines, plagues, and other disasters. Christians also refused to recognize Caesar as a god. In response, Rome persecuted the early church. They tortured Christians and killed them as public spectacle.

In order for the Church to survive, they had to go underground. And they used apocalyptic images for a covert language. Apocalyptic images and idioms were familiar to Jews and Christians, but meant nothing to

---

163. Gentry and others, *Four View on the Book of Revelation*, 38.

Romans. It was the perfect code.

We must take this into consideration when studying Revelation. If we ignore the structure and style of the writing, we will misinterpret it.

"Come Up Here"

John watches these events from Heaven–not earth (God calls him up to heaven to witness the vision, Rev. 4:1-2). This directly affects how we interpret Revelation.

Paul states that, "we do not wrestle against flesh and blood, but against principalities, against powers, against the rulers of the darkness of this age, against spiritual hosts of wickedness in the heavenly places" (Ephesians 6:12). We do not normally see these principalities with the naked eye. But sometimes God allows us to see what is going on in the spirit realm.

John is witnessing the spirit world. And everything he sees may look different as it plays out in the physical world.

For instance, the Red Serpent of Revelation 12 is not a real red serpent. It is a spirit that empowers certain principalities on the earth.

For example, there is a spirit influencing the drug realm. In the natural, we arrest drug dealers all the time. But they keep coming back. In fact, it almost seems like we're fighting Hydra (the mythical snake who regrew two heads every time one was cut off). There is a spirit, or many spirits, empowering the drug world. We will not see success until we deal with the spiritual side of things.

187

The Book of Revelation is John's account of events as seen in the spirit world. He is not watching natural events. He is watching a war in heaven between spirits and principalities. This war affects the natural world, but it is not the natural world. When we understand this, it will give us greater clarity into Revelation.

The Divorce and Judgment of Jerusalem

Revelation is the story of God's divorce of Israel and marriage to the Bride. This imagery enwraps the whole book. The Book of Revelation is not about the end of the world. It is about the establishment of a new world order, the Church.

Some Christians have a hard time believing that God divorced Israel. Because of this, they reject a preterist interpretation of Revelation. Some will say, "God hates divorce," using this as proof that He would never divorce His people.

First, we must remember that the belief that God still has a covenant with Israel is new. For most of church history, theologians understood that the church inherited Israel's place on the earth as God's people. And even though the Jews and Jerusalem have a history with God, they no longer hold a special place in His plans.

Second, God's covenant warned Israel that He would divorce them if they weren't faithful:

"You shall fear the Lord your God and serve Him,.... lest the anger of the Lord your God be aroused against you and destroy you from the face of the earth." (Deut. 6:13, 19)

"Then it shall be, if you by any means forget the Lord your God,.... I testify against you this day that you shall surely perish. As the nations which the Lord destroys before you, so you shall perish, because you would not be obedient to the voice of the Lord your God." (Deut. 8:19-20)

"Because you did not serve the Lord your God with joy and gladness of heart...He will put a yoke of iron on your neck until He has destroyed you." (Deut. 28:47, 48)

The word "destroy" used in these verses means "to exterminate."[164] God says that if the Jews were not faithful, He would wipe them from the face of the planet. He would exterminate their covenant and leave them a wasteland.

Some may point out that God brought judgment against the Jews several times for their lack of faith, but maintained His covenant with them (ex., the Babylonian Captivity). Couldn't the modern state of the Jews reflect a similar situation? But, those examples only prove that God is very slow to resort to such final means. The verses listed above reveal that an ultimate rupture between the Jews and God could occur. The threat that God could divorce His people was an integral part of the old covenant.

---

164. Francis Brown, Samuel Rolles Driver, and Charles Augustus Briggs, *Enhanced Brown-Driver-Briggs Hebrew and English Lexicon* (Oak Harbor, WA: Logos Research Systems, 2000), 1029.

Third, not only did God say that He *could* divorce His people, but we have an example of Him *doing so*: "I gave faithless Israel [the northern ten kingdoms] her certificate of divorce and sent her away because of all her adulteries. Yet I saw that her unfaithful sister Judah had no fear; she also went out and committed adultery" (Jer. 3:8 NIV).

By His own words God states that He divorced Northern Israel for her adulteries. He did this through the Assyrian army, which left northern Israel desolate. He goes on to say that if Judah is not careful, the same fate will befall her.

Finally, in Matthew 23, Jesus declares to Jerusalem that she will be left desolate because of her iniquities:

> "Therefore, indeed, I send you prophets, wise men, and scribes: some of them you will kill and crucify, and some of them you will scourge in your synagogues and persecute from city to city, that on you may come all the righteous blood shed on the earth [land, Gk: '*he ge*'], from the blood of righteous Abel to the blood of Zechariah, son of Berechiah, whom you murdered between the temple and the altar. Assuredly, I say to you, all these things will come upon this generation"[165]

Revelation records this event from the vantage point of heaven. It is the only way that the book makes sense, both to us as a modern audience, and to the original audience two thousand years ago.

From the time of Moses until Jesus, God worked with His people through the "Law and the Prophets." The

---

165. Matthew 23:33-36

Jewish faith stood on God's covenant with them.

The Temple and the sacrificial system were also at the center of their covenant. They needed the sacrificial system to perform their side of the covenant.

When Jerusalem fell, the sacrificial system ended, and with it went ancient Judaism. God wiped it from the face of the planet, just like He said He would.

Only the Pharisees continued with a radical reinterpretation of their faith. The Law and the Torah became so inapplicable to their world that the Jews had to find a way to reinvent themselves. This rebranded version of Judaism became known as Rabbinic Judaism. Rabbinic Judaism looks almost nothing like the Judaism of two thousand years ago.

This is not an argument advocating anti-Semitism. God loves all people. Jesus wept over Jerusalem because He knew what would befall her. And, as we have already stated, God has left a way for the Jews to receive salvation. They can be grafted back into the people of God through Christ. Anti-Semitism is neither biblical nor Christ-like.

As we will see, the Book of Revelation depicts the transfer of covenants. God not only divorced His unfaithful wife, but He married His new Bride, the Church. Revelation promises that the Church will become a shining beacon of hope for the world. It reveals that all wisdom, knowledge, and power will flow from her. And it predicts that she will heal and redeem the nations. Instead of a world nearing destruction, Revelation presents a world on the eve of redemption.

Chapter 2

THE SEVEN SEALS AND

SEVEN TRUMPETS

"After these things I looked, and behold, a door standing open in heaven. And the first voice which I heard was like a trumpet speaking with me, saying, 'Come up here, and I will show you things which must take place after this.' Immediately I was in the Spirit." – Rev. 4:1-2

Thematic Overview

We are skipping the seven letters and jumping straight to John's vision. The seven letters are important, but they do not directly pertain to the bulk of the vision in Revelation.

Starting in Revelation 4, John was taken to heaven, and he was suddenly "in the Spirit." He was having a spiritual vision. He enters the throne room of Jesus and sees a scroll sealed by seven seals. Once the seals are broken, seven trumpets sound. And then seven bowls of wrath are emptied onto "the land." The seals, trumpets, and bowls usually get more attention than the scroll itself. But let's look at Revelation from the apocalyptic genre's point of view.

John employs a heavy amount of apocalyptic reinvestment starting with the scroll. The reinvestment moves backwards through the imagery spanning the bowls of wrath back to the scroll. So every time there is a reinvestment, it is meant to offer more detail and depth to the previous image. We start with the scroll, but everything up through the bowls of wrath ultimately reinvests back into the scroll. It goes as follows: The seven bowls of wrath reinvest back into the seven trumpets. And the seven trumpets reinvest back into the seals. And the seals reinvest back into the scroll. This is classic apocalyptic style.

Yet, there is another theme beautifully intertwined with these apocalyptic reinvestments. In the ancient world, trumpets were used to give commands and make royal announcements. So, once the scroll was opened (the seals), the seven trumpets were Heaven's announcement of what was written in the scroll. Then, seven angels executed what the trumpets announced by pouring out the bowls of wrath. But it all goes back to the scroll. The seals, trumpets, and bowls are all illustrations of what was written on the scroll.

Furthermore, the seals, trumpets, and bowls each have

greater impact than the previous image. The seals burn up one quarter of the land. The trumpets destroy one third. And the bowls consume everything. This technique advances the impact of the previous image, but they are all about the same event.

Thematic Overview of the Book of Revelation

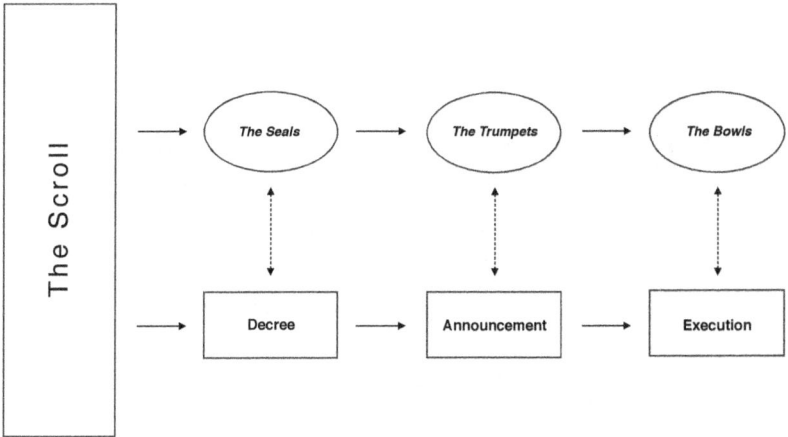

Once we get to Revelation 17, we see another reinvestment. Revelation 16 ends with the destruction of "everything." Then we see the fall of the whore of Babylon and the destruction of the Beast. These images are reinvestments into the bowls of wrath. Which in turn are reinvestments into the trumpets and seals, leading all the way back to the scroll.

Everything revolves around the scroll. Ultimately, every image reinvests back into it. So, the question we need to ask is, "What was in the scroll?"

The scroll was God's certificate of divorce to Israel. Not only does this fit with what happened to Jerusalem in A.D. 70, but Revelation 5 corroborates it. John tells us that no one but the Lamb could open the scroll. Only God had the authority to divorce His wife. No one else could do it.

This is the cornerstone of Revelation. All the cataclysmic imagery utilized throughout the book illustrates this point. Revelation is not about the end of the world. It is about God's divorce from His adulterous wife and His marriage to His new Bride. Failing to understand this will result in an incomplete picture of the book.

The Seven Seals
REVELATION 6:1 – 8:7

The seven seals are the first wave of judgments against Judea. The first four seals release the "four horsemen."

The first horseman is "bent on conquest" (Rev. 6:2-3). This represents the Roman army marching towards Jerusalem. As the Romans progressed through Judea, they conquered everything in their path.

The rider on the red horse took "the peace from the earth [or land]" (Rev. 6:4). Not only was the army marching through Jerusalem, but the *Pax Romana* had ended.

This peace had prevailed for many years throughout the empire. For instance, the historian Epictetus (A.D. 60–140) wrote, "Caesar had obtained for us a profound peace. There are neither wars nor battles" (Discourses 3:13:9). Judea came close to revolt several times during this period, but peace was maintained until A.D. 67.

Then, when Nero died just a year later, turmoil consumed the empire. Many historians thought the empire would not survive. The war with the Jews began a volatile period in Rome's history.

The riders on the black and pale horses represent the famine, pestilence, and death that ensued during the Jewish war. The Roman historians Tacitus, Suetonius, and Josephus documented the horrific fate of the Jews. All these historians record plagues, famines, and catastrophic economic inflation during the war.

The fifth seal revealed martyrs crying out in heaven. They were demanding vengeance for their deaths and torment. "How long, Sovereign Lord, holy and true, until you judge the inhabitants of the earth [land] and avenge our blood?" (Rev. 6:10). The martyrs were not crying out for vengeance all over the world. These are Christians who were persecuted and killed by the Jews. They are asking for God to vindicate them before the Jews and the world. An angel tells them to wait a little while longer. But by the end of Revelation God responds to their cry.

The sixth seal makes the sun dark, turns the moon to blood, and causes the stars to fall from heaven. This is a standard literary technique that used Old Testament imagery to describe the judgment of a city or kingdom. We saw this in Matthew 24 as well. The sixth seal reveals God's judgment against Jerusalem.

Revelation 6:15-16 states that many people would seek refuge in caves to hide from the judgments of God. Josephus records events that fulfill this prophecy. Here is but one example:

> "And on this day the Romans slew all the multitude that appeared openly; but on the following days they searched the hiding places, and **fell upon those that were underground, and in the caverns...**"[166]

This happened many times as the army marched towards Jerusalem. Clearly, we can see how these events fulfilled Revelation 6.

The 144,000 Saints – REVELATION 7:9-17

Revelation 7 introduces a brief pause in the action. John witnesses four angels holding back four winds. The four angels had been granted authority to bring damage to the earth and the sea (Rev. 7:2). So, they are holding back the winds of destruction. They held back the winds until "we have sealed the servants of our God on their foreheads" (Rev. 7:3). Revelation tells us that these saints number 144,000.

---

166. Josephus, *Wars,* 3.7.36

Ancient Jewish culture used symbolism in numbers in a way that we don't in the modern world. The number 1,000 represented the number of quantitative completion or fullness. And we have 1,000 times 12 for the twelve tribes. Yet these are not Jews. They are Christian converts. We know that John believed only Christ-believing Jews were real Jews. Unbelieving Jews were "so-called Jews" that belong to "the synagogue of Satan."[167] So, John would not have called the 144,000 "saints" if they were unconverted Jews. According to John, they are true saints, meaning Christians.

God halts the destruction to "seal" and protect His people within Jerusalem and the surrounding areas.

This happened when Emperor Nero committed suicide in A.D. 68. The Roman generals in charge of putting down the Jewish revolt (Vespasian and Titus) withdrew for a year to secure the empire. This window gave those "sealed" by God a chance to escape the coming destruction. As we saw in Matthew 24, Eusebius records that this happened:

> "But the people of the Church in Jerusalem had been commanded by a revelation, vouchsafed to approved men there before the war, to leave the city and to dwell in a certain town of Perea called Pella. **And when those that believed in Christ had come there from Jerusalem,** then, as if the royal city of the Jews and **the whole land**

---

167. Revelation 2:9

of Judea were entirely destitute of holy men, the judgment of God at length overtook those who had committed
such outrages against Christ and his apostles, and totally
destroyed that generation of impious men."[168]

Epiphanius also recorded that early Christians fled Jerusalem in this window:

"For [Pella] was [the Nazarenes] place of origin, since
all the disciples had settled in Pella after their removal
from Jerusalem—**Christ having told them to abandon
Jerusalem and withdraw from it because of the siege
it was about to under go.**"[169]

Once the Christians fled, Vespasian restored order to the
empire. He then sent Titus back to Judea to subjugate
the Jews.

The seventh seal resulted in silence in heaven for half
an hour. This half hour could have been a literary effect.
It built tension right before the trumpets proclaimed the
judgments in the scroll.

This was the calm before the storm, the moment before
God would announce His divorce from Israel.

168. Eusebius, *Histories*, 3.5.3.

169. Epiphanius, *The Panarion of Epiphanius of Salamis: Book 1,*
trans. Frank Williams (Koninklijke Brill NV, Leiden, The Netherlands: 2009), 129

The Seven Trumpets
REVELATION 8:7 – 11:19

The seven trumpets represent the next round of judgments against Jerusalem. The judgments also begin to look more like the plagues of Egypt. This has a powerful literary effect. It reveals that God now sees Jerusalem as Egypt–the enemy of God and persecutor of His people. John drives this home by directly telling the reader we are discussing Jerusalem: "And their dead bodies will lie in the street of the great city which spiritually is called Sodom and Egypt, where also our Lord was crucified" (Rev. 11:8).

Josephus' eyewitness account of the Jewish war bares a striking resemblance to the trumpets. As the Romans marched towards Jerusalem, they laid waste to Judea to convince them to give up their rebellion. Many battles between the Jews and the Romans broke out, and the Jews were slaughtered. The Romans burned entire villages and killed a countless number of people. The region experienced terrible upheaval. Revelation illustrates something very similar.

After the seventh seal, Revelation records thunder, lightening, and earthquakes in the "land": "Then the angel took the censer, filled it with fire from the altar, and threw it to the earth. And there were noises, thunderings, lightnings, and an earthquake" (Rev. 8:5). These events were a prelude to the coming judgments. Josephus records that such an event took place:

"… There broke out a prodigious storm in the night, with the utmost violence, and very strong winds, with the largest showers of rain, with continual lightnings, terrible thunderings, and amazing concussions and bellowings of the earth, that was in an earthquake. **These things were a manifest indication that some destruction was coming upon men**, when the system of the world was put into this disorder; and **anyone would guess that these wonders foreshowed some grand calamities that were coming.**"[170]

Immediately following these events, the first trumpet sounded. It called for one-third of the trees of the "land" to burn. Josephus records that the Romans set fire to suburbs and villages. For example, he states:

"And, truly, the very view itself of the country was a melancholy thing; for those places which were before adorned with trees and pleasant gardens were now become a desolate country every way, and its trees were all cut down."[171]

The second trumpet destroyed ships and turned the seas to blood.[172] This refers to lives lost during storms or sea battles with the Romans. Josephus records:

---

170. Josephus, *Wars* 4.286-287, emphasis added.

171. Josephus, *Wars* 6.6.

172. Rev. 8:8-9

> "...The greatest part of them [Jews] were carried by the waves, and dashed their ships to pieces against the abrupt parts of the rocks, in so much that the sea was bloody a long way, and the maritime parts were full of dead bodies."[173]

The third trumpet turned the waters poisonous (Rev. 8:10-11). We can assume that this was the dead bodies contaminating the water:

> "One might then see the lake all bloody, and full of dead bodies, for not one of them [Jews] escaped, And a terrible stink, and a very sad sight there was on the following days over that country; for as the shores, they were full of shipwrecks, and of dead bodies all swelled; and as the dead bodies were inflamed by the sun, and putrefied, they corrupted the air."[174]

The fourth trumpet caused the sun, moon, and stars to darken. Once again John uses Biblical imagery to describe Israel's judgment. We have seen this earlier in Revelation and discussed it in Matthew 24.

"One-third" of the heavens darken because the trumpets are an apocalyptic reinvestment of the seals. The seals only saw one-quarter of the land affected by judgment. The trumpets bring "one-third" to emphasize the seals, and to build tension in the story. John employs this imagery again with the bowls of wrath, but to a fuller extent.

---

173. Josephus, *Wars* 3.9.3.

174. Josephus, *Wars* 3.9.5.

The fifth trumpet opened the "bottomless abyss," out of which locusts, smoke, and fire came. The locusts have inspired many interpretations. One of the more interesting ones is that they are helicopters used in the Battle of Armageddon. But many scholars believe that these locusts were demons. Preterists argue that they possessed the inhabitants of Jerusalem during the siege in A.D. 70.

When Jesus came, He came to bring the Kingdom of God and to break the works of the devil, i.e. destroy the kingdom of Satan. This brought a strong demonic counter-response. Part of Jesus' ministry was casting demons out of the Jews. But He warned them that if they did not accept Him, the demons would return sevenfold (Matt. 12:43-45). He was warning Israel that if they did not repent, an even stronger demonic presence would come upon them. The fifth trumpet fulfills that warning.

Revelation 9:5 states that the locusts were not given authority to kill people directly. Only to inwardly torment the Jews [Greek: "*basanizo*"]. To corroborate this, Josephus describes the demonic influence on Jerusalem during the siege:

> "And now, as the city was engaged in a war on all sides, from these treacherous crowds of wicked men, the people of the city, between them, were like a great body torn in pieces... The citizens themselves were under a **terrible consternation and fear**... nor was there ever any occasion for them to leave off their lamentations, because their calamities came perpetually one upon another, although

the **deep consternation** they were in prevented their outward wailing; but, being constrained by their fear to conceal their inward passions, they were **inwardly tormented** [Greek "*basanizo*," same word used in Rev. 9:5], without daring to open their lips in groans."[175]

"But these men, and these only, were incapable of repenting of the wickedness they been guilty of; and separating their souls from their bodies, they used them both as if they belonged to other folks and not to themselves"[176]

They used their bodies as if they weren't their own because they weren't: *they were demonized.*

"They also invented terrible methods of **torment** [noun version of "basanizo" used in Rev 9:5] to discover where any food was... and this was done when these tormentors were not themselves hungry; for the thing had been less barbarous had necessity forced them to it; but this was done to keep their madness in exercise..."[177]

"Neither did any other city ever suffer such miseries, nor did any age ever breed a generation more fruitful in wickedness than this was, from the beginning of the world"[178]

They tortured each other for food. They ate their own children (*Wars* 6.205-208) and *"omitted no method of torment or of barbarity" (Wars 5.1.5).*

---

175. Josephus, *Wars* 5.27-36, emphasis added.

176. Josephus, *Wars* 5.12.4.

177. Josephus, *Wars* 5.435-436, emphasis added.

178. Josephus, *Wars* 5.10.5.

In Deuteronomy, God warned Israel that this would happen if they broke their covenant:

> "They shall besiege you at all your gates until your high and fortified walls, in which you trust, come down throughout all your land; and they shall besiege you at all your gates throughout all your land which the Lord your God has given you. **You shall eat the fruit of your own body, the flesh of your sons and your daughters** whom the Lord your God has given you, in the siege and desperate straits in which your enemy shall distress you.

> "The sensitive and very refined man among you will be hostile toward his brother, toward the wife of his bosom, and toward the rest of his children whom he leaves behind, so that he will not give any of them **the flesh of his children whom he will eat**, because he has nothing left in the siege and desperate straits in which your enemy shall distress you at all your gates.

> "The tender and delicate woman among you, who would not venture to set the sole of her foot on the ground because of her delicateness and sensitivity, will refuse to the husband of her bosom, and to her son and her daughter, her placenta which comes out from between her feet and her children whom she bears; **for she will eat them secretly** for lack of everything in the siege and desperate straits in which your enemy shall distress you at all your gates."[179]

This passage describes Israel's punishment for being unfaithful. That punishment comes in a siege.

---

179. Deuteronomy 28:52-57, emphasis added.

Finally, and returning to Revelation, God allowed the locusts to torment their victims for five months. *The siege of Jerusalem lasted five months.*

The sixth trumpet released four angels to kill a third of mankind. We are told that after they appeared, they immediately became mounted troops:

"The Angel said to the sixth angel who had the trumpet, 'Release the four angels who are bound at the great river Euphrates.' And the four angels who had been kept ready for this very hour and day and month and year were released to kill a third of mankind. The number of the mounted troops was two hundred million. I heard their number."[180]

Amazingly, both Josephus and Tacitus corroborate this. They saw angelic beings in the sky above Judea during the war. Josephus says:

"A few days after that feast... a certain prodigious and incredible phenomenon appeared; I suppose the account of it would seem to be a fable, were it not related by those that saw it, and were not the events that followed it of so considerable a nature as to deserve such signals; for, **before sunsetting, chariots and troops of soldiers in their armor were seen running about among the clouds, and surrounding of cities.**"[181]

---

180. Revelation 9:13-16

181. Josephus, *Wars* 6.296-299.

Josephus claims that people saw heavenly beings in the clouds right before the siege. We know he isn't speaking symbolically because he's afraid his readers wouldn't believe him. He thinks that people will deem this sighting a fable, but he affirms it through eyewitness support.

Furthermore, Tacitus records something similar:

> "Prodigies had occurred... There had been seen hosts joining battle in the skies, the fiery gleam of arms..."[182]

These men were not Christians. There is no evidence that they were familiar with Revelation (nor any reason we should expect them to be). Yet they both saw angelic powers that looked like armies and mounted troops surrounding the cities of Judea, which Revelation predicted.

Revelation also said that these troops totaled two hundred million (Rev. 9:13-16). This is not literal, but instead communicates the incalculable size of the force against Jerusalem.

This passage states that these four angels were stationed on the Euphrates River. Amazingly, to siege Jerusalem, Vespasian took command of four legions that were stationed on the Euphrates River. Josephus records that these were the four legions that sieged Jerusalem. These events are a direct fulfillment of the sixth trumpet in Revelation 9.

---

182. Tacitus, *Histories,* 5.13. Emphasis added.

The Little Book – REVELATION 10

Revelation 10 starts with the strange event of the seven thunders. A large angel appears with a small book. He lifts the little book and cries out to heaven. There are then seven peals of thunder that spoke as words. John moves to write them down, but a voice tells him not to. Though we are not told what they said, we can infer from what happens next.

The angel then raises his voice to heaven and declares that when the seventh trumpet sounds, "the mystery of God would be finished, as He declared to His servants the prophets" (Rev. 10:7).

Jesus declared something similar to His disciples. He said, "to you it has been given to know the mysteries of the Kingdom of God" (Matt. 13:11). This states that the disciples had access to the mysteries of God, to which the prophets had only eluded. Furthermore, Paul states that the Spirit of God now reveals the mysteries of God to us:

> "But we speak the wisdom of God in a mystery, **the hidden wisdom which God ordained before the ages for our glory,** which none of the rulers of this age knew; for had they known, they would not have crucified the Lord of glory. But as it is written: 'Eye has not seen, nor ear heard, Nor have entered into the heart of man The things which God has prepared for those who love Him.' **But God has revealed them to us through His Spirit. For the Spirit searches all things, yes, the deep things of God.**"[183]

---

183. 1 Corinthians 2:7-10, emphasis added.

Jesus' death and resurrection ushered in what the "servants the prophets" had predicted. The deep mysteries of God were made known through Jesus Christ and the Holy Spirit.

This may seem hard to imagine for many, seeing as we do not understand everything about God. But just because something is visible does not mean that we understand it. You can look at the source code for your computer's operating system, but that doesn't mean you understand it.[184]

God gave us His Holy Spirit and thereby opened up the mysteries of the Kingdom. We can access this information through the Spirit (like dreams, prophetic words, visions, etc...). But that doesn't mean we know how to use it. Or even what it means. It is like we have the encyclopedia to everything in the universe sitting on our shelf and we don't even realize it.

John Eats the Book

After the angel makes this declaration, John is told to eat the little book in the angel's hand. The book is sweet to his lips but turns bitter in his stomach. Then he is told "You must prophesy again about many peoples, nations, tongues, and kings" (Rev. 10:11). This passage is an echo of Ezekiel 2:8-10:

---

184. This could be the subject of an entire book, and is. If you want to learn more about this concept, you should read *Secrets to Imitating God* by Bill Johnson.

"But you, son of man, hear what I say to you. Do not be rebellious like that rebellious house; open your mouth and **eat what I give you**.' Now when I looked, there was a hand stretched out to me; and behold, a scroll of a book was in it. Then He spread it before me; and there was writing on the inside and on the outside, and written on it were **lamentations and mourning and woe**. Moreover He said to me, 'Son of man, eat what you find; **eat this scroll, and go, speak to the house of Israel**.' So I opened my mouth, and He caused me to eat that scroll. And He said to me, 'Son of man, feed your belly, and fill your stomach with this scroll that I give you.' So I ate, and it was i**n my mouth like honey in sweetness**... So the Spirit lifted me up and took me away, and **I went in bitterness, in the heat of my spirit**; but the hand of the Lord was strong upon me."[185]

Ezekiel records that he was commissioned to eat a book of "lamentations and mourning and woe" and then prophesy against Israel. At first the scroll was sweet in his mouth, but then it turned bitter in his stomach (it says "in the heat of my spirit," but ancient Jews thought their spirits were in their stomachs). In both cases, the book turns bitter in their stomach because they contain judgments against Israel.

In both instances John and Ezekiel were commissioned to prophesy the destruction of Jerusalem (Ezekiel in the sixth century B.C., and John in the first century A.D.). But John's message contains no future hope for Israel. It only contains hope for the New Jerusalem, which is the Bride, or the Church.

---

185. Ezekiel 2:8-3:3, 3:14, emphasis added.

John then measures the Temple. We know that this is the physical Temple because the gentiles will "tread upon" it. Since this is the actual Temple, this is further evidence that Revelation was written before A.D. 70. Otherwise there would not have been a Temple for John to measure. John is told to measure all parts of the Temple except the outer court, "because it has been given to the gentiles. They will trample on the holy city for 42 months" (Rev. 11:2). This passage should remind us of the Olivet Discourse in Luke:

> "And they will fall by the edge of the sword, and be led away captive into all nations. **And Jerusalem will be trampled by Gentiles until the times of the Gentiles are fulfilled.**"[186]

Both passages predict foreign armies trampling Jerusalem until the "times of the gentiles are fulfilled." The "times of the gentiles" represent the time that the gentiles can rule over God's people. Until the Temple was destroyed, the gentiles could always strike at the heart of Israel's faith. They could dictate when and where Israel worshipped. Once Jesus came, the physical Temple was destroyed and a new Temple was built. This is the Temple of every believer. Because the Temple is now inside of us, non-believers can't restrict our access to it. They can't rule over our faith. Jesus stated:

---

186. Luke 21:24

"Believe Me, the hour is coming when you will neither on this mountain, nor in Jerusalem, worship the Father.... But the hour is coming, and now is, when the true worshipers will worship the Father in spirit and truth; for the Father is seeking such to worship Him. God is Spirit, and those who worship Him must worship in spirit and truth."[187]

Revelation 11:2 states that the gentiles would "tread the holy city underfoot for forty-two months." Then the times of the gentiles would be complete. Formal imperial action against Jerusalem lasted from the spring of A.D. 67 to August of A.D. 70: *forty-two months*.

The Two Witnesses – REVELATION 11

After John measures the Temple, he records that "two witnesses" would be sent to Jerusalem. Heaven gives them the authority to preach. They would wear sackcloth. And they would prophesy 1,260 days, which is forty-two months (Jewish months had 30 days in them). We are not looking at two literal people. Quite often people and objects within the spirit realm are representative of something on earth. The witnesses are also described as "two olive trees" and "two lampstands." We are told they have fire proceeding from their mouths and they have the power to shut the heavens and turn water into blood.

The olive tree represents the source of oil, which is often symbolic of the Holy Spirit and God's anointing.

---

187. John 4:21-24

These witnesses were the source of God's anointing. The lamp stands tell us that they were sources of truth (John often equates truth with light elsewhere in the New Testament). The fire proceeding from their mouths represents the Holy Spirit speaking through them.

They have the ability to shut the heavens and turn water into blood. These images should remind us of Elijah and Moses. Elijah stopped the skies from raining during his ministry and Moses struck the Nile River and turned it to blood. Moses and Elijah were the epitomes of the Law and the Prophets, of which Jesus spoke often. This passage says that the Law and the Prophets prophesied the coming destruction during the war, until Rome destroyed Jerusalem.

We know that God warned His people right up until the end. Josephus records that the period leading up to the Roman siege held many strange and miraculous events. Josephus even states that God attempted to warn His people, but they didn't listen:

> "Now, if any one consider these things, he will find that God takes care of mankind, and by all ways possible foreshows to our race what is for their preservation; but that men perish by those miseries which they madly and voluntarily bring upon themselves."[188]

For instance, Josephus records that a man named Jesus son of Ananus warned the Jews of Jerusalem's destruction:

---

188. Josephus, *Wars*. 6.310

"A voice from the east, a voice from the west, a voice from
the four winds, a voice against Jerusalem and the holy
house, a voice against the bridegrooms and the brides,
and a voice against this whole people!"[189]

Then Jesus son of Ananus' message changed to: "Woe,
woe, to Jerusalem!" (*Wars* 6.306). He chanted this for
seven and a half years. The Jews hated him and often
beat him for it. But he never spoke against those who beat
him, he just kept chanting this message. Josephus says
that he never grew tired, though he did this day and night.
Then, as the siege began, he climbed onto one of the walls
facing the Roman army and declared woe to the city, and
then to himself. At that moment the Romans released a
stone from a siege engine, which struck and killed him.

Tacitus (not a Jew or a Christian) recorded that the
Jews, with hubris, erroneously interpreted these omens
in their favor:

"Prodigies [or warnings] had occurred... There had been
seen hosts joining battle in the skies, the fiery gleam of
arms, the temple illuminated by a sudden radiance from
the clouds. The doors of the inner shrine were suddenly
thrown open, and a voice of more than mortal tone was
heard to cry that the gods were departing [Tacitus was
polytheistic]. At the same instant there was a mighty stir
as of departure... The common people, with the usual
blindness of ambition, had interpreted these mighty destinies of themselves, and could not be brought even by
disasters to believe the truth."[190]

189. Josephus, *Wars* 6.301.

190. Tacitus, *Histories*, 5.13.

Josephus records several other strange warnings as well. He says that a bright light came from the Temple for half an hour during the night, and the Temple area looked as though it was bright as day. Most people saw it as a sign that God was on their side. But Josephus states that the learned among them knew that it predicted their doom (*Wars* 6.290-291). He also described how the Jews chose to ignore other prophetic warnings of their coming destruction:

> "But these men interpreted some of these signals according to their own pleasure; and some of them they utterly despised, until their madness was demonstrated, both by the taking of their city, and their own destruction."[191]

Josephus says that the Jews intentionally reinterpreted "oracles" to their "own pleasure." And that when they were unable to do so, they simply despised them. Their madness drove them to their own destruction.

It seems clear that God actively warned Jerusalem of her coming destruction. Just as Revelation 11 depicted with the two witnesses. But God's warnings were ignored and hated by the Jews.

Revelation also records that the Beast kills the witnesses. Then everyone rejoices at their death. The Beast kills the Law and the Prophets. The Law and Prophets were a representation of true Judaism (Jesus described

---

191. Josephus, *Wars* 6.315

the old testament as the "law and the prophets"). Why would everyone rejoice at the end of Judaism?

Because the Romans did not like the Jews. The Romans respected Judaism because it was ancient. But they thought monotheism was strange and backwards. Furthermore, the Jews caused them problems. They threatened to rebel many times and they never cooperated with Caesar worship. They also never adopted the Roman culture.

"Romanization" was an active part of Rome's imperial strategy. If subservient cultures shifted to Roman culture, they were less likely to revolt. Moreover, everyone from Rome couldn't understand why others didn't want to be Roman. But the Jews rejected all things Roman. They wouldn't adopt their culture and they wouldn't worship their gods. They were a constant thorn in Rome's side. Not only that, but because Jews were scattered all over the Empire, the Jews were not isolated to Jerusalem. They were everywhere, and they were trying to convert Romans to Judaism.

So, when Romans heard that the army had destroyed Jerusalem, many would have rejoiced. It looked as though the Jews wouldn't bother them anymore. Romans hoped that maybe they would finally settle down and Romanize.

But, after the Beast killed the witnesses, the breath of God resurrected them. The witnesses were resurrected in the Church, the true Israel.

The early Christians did not have a New Testament, so they were teaching Christ from the Old Testament, or the Law and the Prophets. In fact, most people couldn't distinguish them from Jews. Romans everywhere thought the two witnesses were gone. But they came back in a new group called "Christians."

Once the two witnesses went to Heaven, there was a great earthquake. Quite often earthquakes represent shifts in the spirit realm. For instance, when Jesus died on the cross, there was an earthquake. Jesus broke the power of sin. This shift was so large that it tore the veil in the Temple and it brought many people back from the dead (Matt. 27:51-53). When Jesus rose from the dead, there was another earthquake (Matt. 28:2).

In Revelation 11, the earthquake represented the Law and the Prophets leaving Jerusalem, and angels being assigned to Jerusalem's destruction. We know there was a powerful shift in the spirit because immediately after this, an angel declared: "The kingdoms of this world have become the kingdoms of our Lord and of His Christ, and He shall reign forever and ever!" (Rev. 11:15). The Law and the Prophets, the power and truth of God's presence, left Israel. God gave it to the Church. And the church was destined to reign with Christ (Rev. 2:26-27; 5:10) until the knowledge of the glory of the Lord covers the earth as the waters cover the sea (Hab. 2:14). The angel was saying that the world belonged to God, and was now the inheritance of His people.

Chapter 3

THE WOMAN AND THE BEAST

Revelation 12 shifts in imagery, but we are still discussing the same event. It just gives us more information. Revelation 4-11 contained the seven seals, the opening of the scroll, and the seven trumpets. This all announced God's divorce from Jerusalem and her judgment.

In Revelation 12, we see another reinvestment into the trumpets and scrolls. We see this two fold spiritual vision elsewhere in the Old Testament. The Pharaoh of Genesis 41 had two dreams with different imagery. But Joseph interprets them as being about the same event. "The dreams of Pharaoh are one; God has shown Pharaoh what He is about to do" (Gen. 41:25).

The seven seals and trumpets build up to the siege of Jerusalem. The events in Revelation 12-14 witness the same period. This shift in perspective reveals a lot about Jerusalem and her relationship to Rome. This information will become important later.

Revelation 12 opens with a woman adorned with a crown of twelve stars and the sun and moon at her feet. This is representative of her power and authority in the spirit world. She is crying out in pain and about to give birth to a child. There is a red dragon with seven heads and ten horns waiting to devour the child. He also strikes down four of the twelve stars around her head. The child is born and heaven snatches Him up before the dragon can devour Him. Then the woman is whisked away into the wilderness for 1,260 days (42 months).

The dragon then starts a war in Heaven. The dragon and his angels fight with Michael and his angels. But Michael defeats the dragon and casts him down to earth. John states that the dragon could not enter Heaven again.

At this point, a loud voice cries stating that Christ's salvation has come and that the dragon can no longer accuse the brethren. The serpent is identified as Satan later (Rev. 12:9). Revelation then tells us that the dragon attempts to persecute the woman, but the woman is protected. This further enrages the dragon, which then turns to make war against the saints.

Identifying the Woman, Child, and Serpent

Many believe that the woman is either the Roman Catholic Church or Mary, because she gives birth to the Child, who is Jesus. But the woman's ornaments appear to identify her as Israel.

She has twelve stars on her crown. This should remind

us of the twelve tribes of Israel. She also stands on the sun and moon. She is a woman of great power and favor. Even though Rome ruled over Israel, she had favor with Rome. Josephus said this about her:

> "...It had so come to pass, that **our city Jerusalem had arrived at a higher degree of felicity than any other city under the Roman government**."[192]

> She was the only province that Rome exempted from various imperial edicts. They did not have to place a statue of Caesar in their Temple. They did not have to swear that Caesar was "Lord of Lords, and King of Kings." And Rome allowed Israel to maintain her monotheism.

The Child is Jesus and the Kingdom of God. Quite often kings and their kingdoms are interchangeable in prophetic images. In Matthew 24, Jesus describes the destruction of Jerusalem as "birth pangs." Revelation tells us that the woman is experiencing pain as she gives birth.

After Jerusalem was destroyed, Jesus and the Kingdom of God were vindicated before Israel. The period between Jesus' birth and her destruction was turbulent for Jerusalem. It culminated in the war with Rome. The woman in Revelation 12 is giving birth to the Kingdom, and it is causing her great pain.

The dragon is the only person Revelation identifies. Satan attempts to destroy the Messiah and the Kingdom,

---

192. Josephus, *Wars* 1.11, emphasis added.

but fails. Then he wages war in Heaven against Michael. He fails and Michael throws him back to earth. Satan then attempts to destroy Israel, but he can't. Jerusalem was protected between the time of Jesus' death and her destruction.

Caligula attempted to wipe out the Jews, but he died before he could go through with his plan. Satan tried to inspire Rome to destroy Israel. But He couldn't. So, He turned Rome towards the church. The first great Roman persecution started in A.D. 64 and lasted for 42 months (the amount of time the woman was protected in the wilderness).

The Beast
REVELATION 13

Now we come to the Beast. There have been thousands of attempts to identify the Beast. Starting in the second century, Christians have claimed that they were in the final days before the apocalypse. The only thing we can say about these teachers is that none of them have been right.

With the Beast, John turns from Israel and to the Roman Empire–the instrument of Israel's final judgment. John issues both a warning and a comfort. It is a warning to Christians about Nero's persecution. It comforts Christians because is says that God will use the Beast to vindicate the Church.

Many ancient and modern scholars believe that the Beast represented the Roman Empire and Emperor Nero.

Revelation depicts two beasts, not one. But, the second beast acted like and exercised all the authority of the first beast. This seems to be a mix of apocalyptic symbolism and real events.

The beast has character traits of the dragon. This is because Satan inspired the Beast. Satan worked through the Roman Empire when he attempted to devour the woman, and when he turned on the Church. Here are the reasons why Rome and Nero fit the description of the Beast.

The Beast arises from the sea, which, from the perspective of Jerusalem, was the geographical location of Rome. The second beast comes out of the ground, representing Rome's resurrection (see below).

The Beast was given great power (Rev. 13:2). The Roman Empire was the most powerful entity in the world. Nothing could stand in its path.

The Beast was evil and blasphemed against God. The Romans considered many of their emperors gods, and Nero was no different. He called himself "the new Apollo," "Almighty God" and "Savior." He killed Christians for not worshipping him as a god.

An angel tells us that the seven heads of the Beast represent both seven mountains and seven kings (Rev. 17: 9-10). The seven mountains refer to the seven hills that surround the city of Rome. These hills were well known in the ancient world. They were like Rome's White House, or Statue of Liberty. People knew what they represented.

The seven kings resemble the first seven emperors of

Rome. An angel tells John that the first five of the horns have fallen. One is still alive. And one is yet to come, but he will only remain a little while (Rev. 17:7). The first 7 emperors of Rome go as follows: Julius, Augusts, Tiberius, Gaius (Caligula), Claudius, Nero, and Galba. The first five of these "have fallen," meaning they died before the writing of Revelation. Nero was the sixth emperor and still alive. The seventh emperor, Galba, came shortly after Nero's death. But he only lived for seven months (he only remained a little while). These emperors were all loosely related. But once Galba died, the Flavian family took over the throne, ending the first line of emperors.

Revelation records that the Beast made war with the saints for 42 months (Rev. 13:5-7). Nero started the first great persecution of Christianity in A.D. 64. These persecutions were terrible. He had Christians torn limb from limb by wild animals. He also used them as human torches for palace parties. Nero's persecution lasted exactly 42 months (November of A.D. 64 – June of A.D. 68).

Revelation implies that the Beast dies and then returns to life. This corresponds with events in the late 60s A.D.. In A.D. 68, Nero committed suicide. Ancient historians record that Rome was in a state of upheaval during Nero's reign. But when Nero died, that upheaval turned to chaos. Many thought the empire would collapse.

Josephus records that the empire was near "ruin" (*Wars* 7.4.2). Tacitus said this period was "rich with disasters, terrible battles, torn by civil struggles, horrible even in peace. Four emperors were felled by the sword; there were three civil wars, more foreign wars and often both at the same time" (*Histories* 1.2). In modern times, it would be like four consecutive presidential assassinations. Florida, California, and Texas entering open revolt, and China invading–all at the same time. Everyone would think that the United States had collapsed. It would be difficult to imagine coming back from such chaos. But, to everyone's surprise, Rome did.

The Roman historian Suetonius writes: "The empire, which for a long time had been unsettled and, as it were, drifting through the usurpation and violent death of three emperors, was at last taken in hand and given stability by the Flavian family."

Josephus states that Vespasian's government unexpectedly delivered Rome from ruin (*Wars* 4.11.5). To many, Rome appeared to have died and then returned again to life. When the Beast "died" the war with the Jews was paused. But when the Beast "resurrected," it brought about a renewed campaign against Jerusalem.

The Mark of the Beast

When John mentions the mark of the beast, he hints that he is speaking in code. This should give us some clues as to what he meant:

> "Here is wisdom. Let him who has understanding calculate the number of the beast, for it is the number of a man: His number is 666."[193]

---

193. Revelation 13:18

John is saying, "Pay attention, use your brain, and you will know who the beast is." In ancient Greek and Hebrew, letters doubled as numbers. Alpha=1, beta=2, etc... Since each letter had a numeric value, words had numeric values as well. This is the secret "code" John employed. This would have meant nothing to the Romans (Latin did not do this), but it would have made sense to attentive Christians.

When you spell out Emperor Neron ("Neron" was the more common way of spelling his name) in Greek, and then translate it into Hebrew, the letters add up to 666.

Some scholars–even the early church historian Ireneaus[194]–recognized that many names could add up to 666. So, this was not proof that Nero was the Antichrist in and of itself.

But, the most compelling support for Nero as the Beast comes from textual variants of Revelation. Some early manuscripts of Revelation recorded that the mark of the beast was 616, not 666. At first this may seem like it was a "typo" by early transcribers. But, in Greek, you can spell Nero two ways: Emperor Nero, or Emperor Neron. Both were acceptable, though Neron was more common. What's surprising is that when you translate these into Hebrew, Emperor Neron adds up to 666 and Emperor Nero adds up to 616. This indicates that John and the early church understood the Beast to be Emperor Nero (and Rome).[195]

---

194. Irenaeus, *Against Heresies*, 5.30.3.

195. Steven McKenzie, *How to Read the Bible: History, Prophecy, Literature* (New York, NY: Oxford University Press, 2005), 143.

Chapter 4

THE FINAL JUDGMENT OF ISRAEL

Revelation 14 begins with a buildup to Jerusalem's final judgment. But before the angels release the bowls of wrath, John sees 144,000 saints sealed by God.

These are Christians whom the Romans and Jews killed through persecutions. Rome killed them because they resisted the Beast.

The Jews killed them because they did not convert back to Judaism. Or as Revelation puts it, because they had not been defiled "by the woman [Jerusalem], for they were virgins" (Rev.14:4). These are not the same 144,000 that we saw earlier.

Those 144,000 saints were alive. They got a chance to flee Jerusalem before it was destroyed. The 144,000 John sees in Revelation 14 had died.

Proclamations of the End – REVELATION 14:6-13

Next, we witness three angels making three declarations:

1. "Then I saw another angel flying in the midst of heaven, having the everlasting gospel to preach to those who dwell on the earth to every nation, tribe, tongue, and people — saying with a loud voice, '*Fear God and give glory to Him, for the hour of His judgment has come; and worship Him who made heaven and earth, the sea and springs of water.*'"[196]

2. "And another angel followed, saying, '*Babylon is fallen, is fallen, that great city, because she has made all nations drink of the wine of the wrath of her fornication.*'"[197]

3. "Then a third angel followed them, saying with a loud voice, '*If anyone worships the beast and his image, and receives his mark on his forehead or on his hand, he himself shall also drink of the wine of the wrath of God, which is poured out full strength into the cup of His indignation.*'"[198]

---

196. Revelation 14:6-7, emphasis added.

197. Revelation 14:8

198. Revelation 14:9-11

This is the beginning of the end for Jerusalem. The first angel declares that the hour of judgment has come. The seals have been broken. The trumpets have announced the coming destruction. And soon those orders will be poured out in the seven bowls of wrath.

The second angel states that Babylon has fallen. Revelation again refers to Jerusalem with the name of a former enemy of God.

The final angel urges people not to worship the Beast, so that people do not suffer the same judgment as him.

The Grapes of Wrath– REVELATION 14:14-20

Revelation 14:14-16 depicts Jesus reaping the grapes of wrath. The ripe fruit represents Israel and her judgment. They are ripe because the time of her judgment has come. An angel gathers the "fruit" and throws it into the winepress of God's wrath:

> "Thrust in your sharp sickle and gather the clusters of the vine of the earth, for her grapes are fully ripe." So the angel thrust his sickle into the earth and gathered the vine of the earth, and threw it into the great winepress of the wrath of God."[199]

This judgment is location specific. It is not global. Revelation gives us clues as to its location:

---

199. Revelation 14:18-19

> "And they were trampled in the winepress outside of the city, and blood came out of the winepress, up to the horses' bridles, for 1,600 stadia."

Revelation records that the bloodshed will cover an area of 1,600 stadia. A stadia was a unit of Roman measurement. The *Itenerarum of Antonius of Piacenza* recorded that the Roman province of Palestine was 1,664 stadia in length.[200] Judea is in Palestine. Revelation says that judgment would fully consume Israel, and that her blood would fill the entire region.

Josephus describes this in great detail. For example: "the sea was bloody a long way, and the maritime parts were full of dead bodies" (*Wars* 3.426). "One might then see the lake all bloody, and full of dead bodies, for not one of them escaped" (*Wars* 3.529). "The country through which they had fled was filled with slaughter, and Jordan could not be passed over, by reason of the dead bodies that were in it, but because the lake Asphaltitis was also full of dead bodies, that were carried down into it by the river" (Wars 4.437). "And now the outer temple was all of it overflowed with blood; and that day, as is came on, saw eight thousand five hundred dead bodies there." (*Wars* 4.313). "And the blood of all sorts of dead carcasses stood in lakes and in the holy courts themselves" (*Wars* 5.18). He also recorded this:

---

200. Robert Mounce, *The Book of Revelation* (Eerdmand Publishing Company, Grand Rapids, MI:1998), 218. See note 45.

"...when they [the Roman soldiers] went in numbers into the lanes of the city, with their swords drawn, they slew those whom they overtook, without mercy, and set fire to the houses wither the Jews were fled, and burnt every soul in them, and laid waste a great many of the rest; .... and [the Romans] made the whole city run down with blood, to such a degree indeed that the fire of many of the houses was quenched with these men's blood."[201]

The seas and rivers were full of dead bodies and blood. Entire villages were razed to the ground. The Romans killed everyone in their path. Jerusalem had so much blood running in the streets that it put out fires in the city. There were eight and a half thousand bodies in the Temple alone. This was a direct fulfillment of Revelation 14:20.

The Seven Bowls
REVELATION 16

As we move forward, we come to the climax of Israel's judgment: the seven bowls of wrath. There is a strong correlation between the bowls and the plagues of Egypt. But this should not surprise us. In Deuteronomy, God warned the Jews that He would bring the plagues of Egypt upon them if they were unfaithful: "Moreover He will bring back on you all the diseases of Egypt" (Deut. 28:60). The bowls of wrath are a fulfillment of that promise.

The Jews received sores (Rev. 16:2). Water turned to

---

201. Josephus, *Wars*, 6.404-7

blood (Rev. 16:3-7). The sun scorched them (Rev. 16:8-9; the blight of Egypt). And the sun went dark (Rev. 16:10-11). Some Jews recognized their fate. Yet, in their madness they did not repent. Instead, they cursed God and His laws (Rev. 16:9, 11). Josephus records that they did just this:

> "These men, therefore, trampled upon all the laws of man, and laughed at the laws of God; and for the oracles of the prophets, they ridiculed them as the tricks of jugglers."[202]

As we approach the climactic destruction of Jerusalem, the sixth bowl records Jesus' warning:

> "'Behold, I am coming as a thief. Blessed is he who watches, and keeps his garments, lest he walk naked and they see his shame.' And they gathered them together to the place called in Hebrew, Armageddon."[203]

This is similar to Jesus' warning in Matthew 24. There, He declared that He would come like a thief in the night. We must capture the feel of this moment in history.

The Jews have suffered terrible defeats throughout the war. The siege had claimed countless lives and reduced them to demonic barbarity. The Romans destroyed many of the towers and walls. They are making their way into

---

202. Josephus, *Wars*, 4.386

203. Revelation 16:15-16

the outer city. To many, this is the 11th hour when God is supposed to come to their rescue. This is where He shows the world His wonderful works through the salvation of Israel. The Messiah should rise up at any moment. Angels should appear in the heavens, and the gentiles should tremble. This is what the Jews expected. This is not what happened.

The Messiah came, but not in the way that they had hoped.

John says that they will be gathered in "Armageddon." To the Jews, this would have been painfully ironic. Armageddon is the Greek transliteration of the Hebrew "Har Megiddo." This translates as Mount Megiddo.

Mount Megiddo is a real place in Israel and held a special, yet tragic significance to the Jews. It is where their beloved king Josiah fought against the Egyptians and died (circa 609 B.C.).

Josiah was one of the few good kings of Judah. In fact, apart from David, he was the best one they had. He restored the practices of the Law. He tore down every altar to foreign gods. He brought about a mini-revival in Jerusalem and turned the Jews back to God. When Necho, the Pharaoh of Egypt, wished to pass through Judah to war against Babylon, Josiah refused him. A battle ensued and everyone expected Josiah to be victorious. Since he had upheld the covenant and restored the Law, they expected God to grant him victory over their enemies.

Therefore, Josiah's death and Judah's defeat were devastating and unexpected. At this point, God had declared that their judgment would no longer be held back.[204] This marked the end of Jerusalem's independence. It came under Egyptian rule, and 30 years later it fell to Babylon, ushering in the Babylonian Captivity.

The Battle of Megiddo would have held special meaning to the Jews. It would have signified that there comes a time when nothing can stop their judgment. So, when Jesus stated that He would gather them together at Mount Megiddo, He was saying that their hopes of salvation would not come. Just as they hadn't with Josiah.

Finally, we crescendo to the climax with the seventh bowl:

> "Then the seventh angel poured out his bowl into the air, and a loud voice came out of the temple of heaven, from the throne, saying, 'It is done!' And there were noises and thunderings and lightnings; and there was a great earthquake, such a mighty and great earthquake as had not occurred since men were on the earth."[205]

Jesus declares, "It is done!" Jerusalem has been judged for her crimes. God had divorced His first wife and sentenced her to death. There was a large earthquake signifying this monumental transition of power.

To further illustrate that we are discussing Jerusalem, John records that the "great city," "Babylon" was divided

---

204. See Jeremiah 7:16; 11:14; 14:12.

205. Revelation 16:17-18

into three parts, which aided her fall (Rev. 16:19). Josephus recorded that Jerusalem was broken into three parts: "And now there were three treacherous factions in the city, the one parted from the other" (Wars 5.21). Josephus goes on to describe how these three factions warred with each other. And when the Romans finally breached the walls, these factions killed each other and innocent Jews as they retreated through the city.

God's Punishment For Adultery

As the repercussions of the seventh bowl rattled through Judea, John records that great hailstones fell from heaven and struck Jerusalem: "And great hail from heaven fell upon men, each hailstone about the weight of a talent." (Rev. 16:21). John is describing the final punishment for Jerusalem's adultery. God's punishment for adultery is stoning (Lev. 20:10), which Revelation 16:21 describes.

The Jews had rejected God's prophets, His Son, and His people. For this, Jerusalem was stoned for her adultery and unfaithfulness. When God offered them complete redemption, they turned away and chose to follow their own path. Josephus records a literal fulfillment of their punishment when the Romans used catapults in their siege against Jerusalem:

> **"Now, the stones that were cast were of the weight of a talent,** and were carried two furlongs and farther. The blow they gave was no way to be sustained, not only by

those that stood first in the way, but by those that were beyond them for a great space."[206]

The Romans hurled large stones at Jerusalem. These stones were the same size as the ones described in Revelation 16:21. This is a direct fulfillment of Revelation 16:21. After the Romans pounded the city, they took it. They killed many, set fire to most of the city, destroyed the Temple, and scattered the survivors around the empire. This was Jerusalem's judgment and punishment. She was divorced and "put away."

---

206. Josephus, *Wars,* 5.270, emphasis added.

Chapter 5

THE PROSTITUTE AND THE BRIDE

"Then one of the seven angels... came to me and talked with me, saying, 'Come, I will show you the bride, the Lamb's wife.' And he carried me away in the Spirit to a great and high mountain, and showed me the great city, the holy Jerusalem, descending out of heaven from God, having the glory of God." – Rev. 21:9-11

Once we reach Revelation 17, John takes another step back to look at these events from another perspective. This is more apocalyptic reinvestment. This part of scripture reveals the divorce of Jerusalem from a different vantage point.

The Beast and the woman return, but she is now called "Babylon." This is the same woman who fled into the wilderness after giving birth in chapter 12. The woman loses her protection from the beast and he devours her. Which is exactly what happened to Jerusalem.

The Woman and The Beast – Part 2
REVELATION 17

Chapter 17 begins with a picture of the prostitute on the back of the beast:

> "The woman was arrayed in purple and scarlet, and adorned with gold and precious stones and pearls, having in her hand a golden cup full of abominations and the filthiness of her fornication. And on her forehead a name was written:
>
> MYSTERY,
> BABYLON THE GREAT,
> THE MOTHER OF ALL PROSTITUES
> AND OF THE ABOMINATIONS OF THE EARTH
>
> I saw the woman, drunk with the blood of the saints and with the blood of the martyrs of Jesus."[207]

Some believe that the woman is Rome because she sits on seven hills (Rev. 17:9). But it is more likely that she is Jerusalem.

First, the woman is described as "the great city" (Rev. 17:18). John refers to Jerusalem as "the great city" several other times throughout Revelation (17:18; 14:8; 16:19; 18:10; 16, 21). As an example, Revelation 11:8 says that "the great city" is the city where "our Lord was crucified."

---

207. Revelation 17:4-6

Second, John uses imagery from Jerusalem's destruction in the sixth century B.C.. In Jeremiah 3, God divorces the northern kingdoms of Israel: "I gave faithless Israel her certificate of divorce and sent her away because of all her adulteries. Yet I saw that her unfaithful sister Judah had no fear; she also went out and committed adultery." (Jer. 3:8, NIV). God divorced northern Israel when Assyria destroyed them, but spared Judah. Revelation records that the prostitute would suffer the same fate (Rev. 17:16; 19:2).

Jeremiah said that Judah's wickedness "defiled the land" (LXX Gk, "*he ge*," Jer. 3:1-2, 9). Revelation 19:2 states that the woman "corrupted the earth [or land, Gk, "*he ge*"]" with her "fornications."

Jeremiah declared that Judah had "a harlot's forehead" (Jer. 3:3). The prostitute in Revelation has "BABYLON THE GREAT, THE MOTHER OF ALL PROSTITUTES" (Rev. 17:5, NIV) inscribed upon her head. The similarity in language leads us to conclude that John is discussing Jerusalem by harkening back to her past.

Third, the woman drank "the blood of prophets and of the saints, and of all who have been killed on the earth [or land, Gk, "*he ge*"]" (Rev. 18:24). Some might believe this indicates that the woman is Rome, because of the Roman persecutions. But by A.D. 70, the Romans had only just begun to persecute Christians. Throughout the New Testament the Jews are the ones persecuting the saints, not Rome. Additionally, Rome had not killed any of the prophets. This is unique to Jerusalem and the Jews.

In fact, it is for this sin that Jesus declared Jerusalem's desolation:

> "Therefore, indeed, **I send you prophets, wise men, and scribes: some of them you will kill and crucify**, and some of them you will scourge in your synagogues and persecute from city to city, that on you may come all the righteous blood shed on the earth [land, Gk: 'he ge'], from the blood of righteous Abel to the blood of Zechariah, son of Berechiah, whom you murdered between the temple and the altar. **Assuredly, I say to you, all these things will come upon this generation.**"[208]

Also see Luke:

> "Therefore the wisdom of God also said, 'I will send them prophets and apostles, and some of them they will kill and persecute,' that the blood of **all the prophets** which was shed from the **foundation of the world** may be required of this generation, from the blood of Abel to the blood of Zechariah who perished between the altar and the temple. **Yes, I say to you, it shall be required of this generation.**"[209]

Jesus said that Jerusalem would be destroyed for every prophet, apostle, and saint that she killed. Throughout Revelation, Jesus judges those who killed Him and persecuted His people. This forces us to conclude that we are discussing Jerusalem.

---

208. Matthew 23:24-36, emphasis added.

209. Luke 11:50-51, emphasis added.

Furthermore, the Jews called down judgment on themselves. During Jesus's trial, Pilate attempted to set Jesus free. He didn't want Jesus' blood on his hands. To which the Jews responded: "Let His blood be on us and on our children!" (Matt. 27:25).

Additionally, John records that the prostitute thought she was safe from judgment because she was a queen: "I am a queen, I am not a widow, I will experience no sorrow" (Rev. 18:7). But she will experience sorrow: "Therefore her plagues will come in one day—death and mourning and famine. And she will be utterly burned with fire, for strong is the Lord God who judges her" (Rev. 18:8). This again directs the reader back to Jeremiah and previous judgments laid against Jerusalem.

First, Jerusalem saw herself as queen. God was the King of the nations: "Who would not fear You, O King of the nations?" (Jer. 10:7). She was married to him and His thrown was in Jerusalem (see Jer. 3:14; 14:21). Therefore, she was His queen.

Because of her position in Heaven, she thought she was immune from judgment:

"Yet you say, 'Because I [Jerusalem] am innocent, Surely His anger shall turn from me.' Behold, I will plead My case against you, Because you say, 'I have not sinned.'" (Jer. 2:35)

Because of her unfaithfulness and her arrogance, God brought swift destruction upon her by the hands of the Babylonians.

Revelation 18 mirrors the same thing for Jerusalem in the first century. The Jews thought they still had a covenant with God. And in her arrogance she thought she was innocent. Even though Rome was at her gates, she believed her King would rescue her. But He didn't.

The fact that she couldn't see her fate is part of the reason why "mystery" was written on her head. The Jews were God's people. They should have been able to identify the Messiah. But instead, they killed Him and persecuted His people. Moreover, her arrogance and pride caused her to believe that she was safe from judgment. How she came to this conclusion is a mystery.

Lamentations used similar language to describe Jerusalem's first fall: "How lonely sits the city that was full of people! How like a widow is she, who was great among the nations! The princess among the provinces Has become a slave!" (Lamentations 1:1). In a spiritual sense, Jerusalem did rule over the rest of the world, and she was waiting for that reality to manifest on the earth. Unfortunately for her, it never did.

Next, the prostitute wears the colors of a Jewish Priest: "The woman was arrayed in purple and scarlet, and adorned with gold and precious stones and pearls, having in her hand a golden cup full of abominations and the filthiness of her fornication" (Rev. 17:4). The priests wore an ephod and a breastplate that were made of "gold, blue, purple, and scarlet thread, and fine woven linen, artistically worked." (Ex. 28:6,15).

The High Priest wore a golden plate that read:

"HOLINESS TO THE LORD." This title was to "always be on [Aaron's] forehead, that [the offerings of Israel] may be accepted before the LORD" (Ex. 28:38). Yet, the prostitute has "THE MOTHER OF ALL PROSTITUTES AND OF THE ABOMINATIONS OF THE EARTH" inscribed upon her forehead. This clearly contrasts her priestly call with her adulterous activity. The prostitute's grand description is also reminiscent of the appearance of the Temple.[210]

Finally, there is a powerful contrast between the prostitute and the new bride that cements the prostitute's identity as Jerusalem.

The Prostitute and the Bride

Revelation 17 and 21 form a striking positive/negative contrast between the adulterous Jerusalem and the chaste Bride. John calls the Bride the "New Jerusalem," asking the reader to compare her to the old. Elsewhere in Revelation, John describes the old Jerusalem as "Sodom and Egypt" (Rev. 11:8) and "Babylon" (Rev. 17). These names cast her as the enemy of God. There is a cruel irony in this. Instead of conducting herself as the faithful bride of God, Jerusalem has become His enemy.

This old/new Jerusalem comparison between Judaism and the Church is not new to the New Testament. In Galatians, Paul states that the Jerusalem on earth is

210. Josephus, *Wars* 5.222-3.

currently under bondage (Gal. 4:25), yet the "Jerusalem above is free, which is the mother of us all" (4:25). He calls the Church the "Jerusalem above." In Revelation, John sees the New Jerusalem "descending from heaven" (i.e., from above). Revelation's contrast between the new and old Jerusalem roots the prostitute of Revelation 17 as Jerusalem, God's unfaithful bride.

Consider how Revelation describes the two women:

1) An angel introduces the prostitute and the Bride with the same language:

Revelation 17:1-2: *"Then one of the seven angels who had the seven bowls came and talked with me, saying to me, "Come, I will show you the judgment of the great harlot who sits on many waters, with whom the kings of the earth committed fornication, and the inhabitants of the earth [or land, Gk, "he ge,"] were made drunk with the wine of her fornication."*

Revelation 21:9: *"Then one of the seven angels who had the seven bowls filled with the seven last plagues came to me and talked with me, saying, "Come, I will show you the bride, the Lamb's wife."*

2) The two women have contrasting characters:

Revelation 17:1b: *"Come, I will show you the judgment of the great harlot who sits on many waters"*

Revelation 21:9b, 10b*: "Come, I will show you the bride, the Lamb's wife... having the glory of God"*

3) The women are in contrasting environments:

Revelation 17:3b: *"So he carried me away in the Spirit into the wilderness. And I saw a woman sitting on a scarlet beast..."*

Revelation 21:10-11: *"And he carried me away in the Spirit to a great and high mountain, and showed me the great city, the holy Jerusalem, descending out of heaven from God, having the glory of God."*

We see the prostitute in the wilderness (where the woman of Revelation 12 fled). But the Bride is exalted upon a high mountain. She also descends from heaven, carrying the glory of God.

Furthermore, the prostitute's position on the back of the Beast illustrates dependence on Rome rather than her identity with Rome. Dr. Kenneth Gentry describes the implications of this imagery very well:

"The image reminds us of Israel's past dependence on Rome so she could attack Christ and his followers. Josephus writes: 'It seems to me to be necessary here to give an account of all the honors the Romans and their emperors paid to our nation, and of the leagues of mutual assistance they have made with it' (Antiquities 14.10.1-2).

Using this leverage ("we have no king but Caesar," John 19:15), the Jews demanded Christ's crucifixion (Matt. 23:37-39; John 19:12-16) and constantly agitated against the Christians so as to involve the Romans in their persecution (Acts 4:27; 16:20; 17:7; 18:12; 21:11; 24:1-9; 25:1-2). 'And they began to accuse him, saying 'We have found this man subverting our nation. He opposes payment of taxes to Caesar and claims to be Christ, a king'" (Luke 23:2). But now Jerusalem's former ally against Christ turns and destroys her (Rev. 18:16)."[211]

As Dr. Gentry points out, the Jews not only had favor with Rome, but she often appealed to Rome as an ally against Christians. But Revelation records that the Beast turned on the prostitute and devoured her. And in A.D. 67, Rome turned on Jerusalem and destroyed her

The Fate of Babylon – REVELATION 18-19

Revelation 18 – 19 combines imagery from many Old Testament judgments to paint a graphic picture of Jerusalem's fall. Revelation compares her judgment to those of Babylon, Tyre, and her first judgment in the sixth century B.C.. Here are but a few examples:

1) Revelation 18:1 states: "After these things I saw another angel coming down from heaven, having great authority, and the earth was illuminated with his glory."

---

211. Gentry and others, *Four View on the Book of Revelation*, 78-79.

This is a reference to Ezekiel: "And behold, the glory of the God of Israel came from the way of the east. His voice was like the sound of many waters; and the earth shone with His glory." (Ez. 43:2) In this vision, God told Ezekiel that He would judge Jerusalem for her sins (43:3). This is a direct reference to Jerusalem's judgment in the sixth century B.C..

2) The same angel declares, "Babylon the great is fallen, is fallen!" He repeats this phrase throughout this section of Revelation. Isaiah records the judgment of the first Babylon with nearly identical language: "Then he answered and said, 'Babylon is fallen, is fallen!'" (Is. 21.9). Revelation associates Jerusalem's destruction with the judgment of Babylon – the enemy of God's people.

3) In the same verse, the angel says that the prostitute "has become a dwelling place of demons, a prison for every foul spirit, and a cage for every unclean and hated bird!" As we have already discussed, Jerusalem became severely demonized during the siege. The Jews were reduced to barbarity, fulfilling the first part of this declaration. Josephus records that during the siege, bodies were left to rot in the streets, which attracted birds the Mosaic Law considered "unclean":

> "But these zealots came at last to that degree of barbarity, as not to bestow a burial either on those slain in the city, or on those that lay along the roads… they left the dead bodies to putrefy under the sun."[212]

---

212. Josephus, *Wars,* 4.381-82

This too was the fate of the original Babylon (Is. 14:23).

(4) Revelation 18:3 states that the prostitute made the nations "drunk with her fornications." Many believers think that she can't be Jerusalem because she did not have this kind of influence. But this is a direct reference to the original Babylon's fall in Jeremiah 51:7. The original Babylon didn't make the whole world drunk either. Revelation applies this imagery to Jerusalem for literary effect.

(5) Revelation 18:8 indicates that the prostitute's fall would come "in one day." Again, we see a reference to the first Babylon. Isaiah prophesies that her destruction would come in one day as well: "But these two things shall come to you in a moment, in one day: The loss of children, and widowhood." (Is. 47:9) This language illustrates the suddenness and totality of Jerusalem's judgment.

(6) Revelation 18:4 records that an angel called God's people out of Babylon so that they wouldn't suffer her fate. This occurred when there was a gap in the war and Christians were able to flee Judea.

(7) There are direct allusions to Egypt's judgment as recorded in Exodus. Revelation 18:5 states: "For her [Babylon/Jerusalem] sins have reached to heaven, and God has remembered her iniquities." This is a mirror of God's statement when He delivered Israel out of Egypt: "Then the children of Israel groaned because of the bondage, and they cried out; and their cry came up to God because of the bondage. So God heard their groaning, and God remembered His covenant with Abraham, with Isaac, and with Jacob" (Ex. 2:23-24).

In Revelation, we see a stark contrast between their bondage under Pharaoh and their current plight under Rome. In Exodus, Israel's cry for help came to heaven and God remembered His covenant with them. In Revelation, Israel's sins reached up to God and God remembered her iniquities. This imagery only has power if the prostitute is Jerusalem.

God's call for His people to come out of Babylon in Revelation 18:4 is also a twist on the Exodus story. Not only does God judge Jerusalem as He did Egypt, but He also calls His true people out of her, just as He did in Exodus. Yet Israel is now the one who has hardened her heart against God, not Pharaoh.

Babylon's Fall – REVELATION 18:9 – 24

Starting in verse 9, the kings and the merchants of the "earth" weep over Babylon's fall. Some may object and say that the kings nor the merchants of the world mourned Jerusalem's fall. And that a modern day superpower would fit this description better.

But this verse doesn't say world, it says land (Gk, "*he ge*"). Jerusalem was the economic and political hub of Palestine. Her destruction would have caused dramatic economic and political convulsions in the region. This would have caused the local leaders and merchants to mourn her fall.

In Revelation 18:20, an angel shouts: "Rejoice over her, O heaven, and you holy apostles and prophets, for God has avenged you on her!" (Rev. 18:20). In Revelation 6, we witnessed martyred saints crying out for vengeance. An angel told them to "rest" and be patient, and that their prayers would be answered at the appointed time. Revelation 18:20 answers that prayer. They have been avenged. This links the latter part of Revelation to the events at the beginning of this vision.

Heaven then celebrates Babylon's fall, announcing God's marriage to His new Bride, "Let us be glad and rejoice and give Him glory, for the marriage of the Lamb has come, and His wife has made herself ready".[213]

---

213. Revelation 19:7

Chapter 6

THE WEDDING FEAST OF THE BRIDE

Revelation 19 takes a turn towards the hopeful as we discuss the Bride. The previous fifteen chapters have described Jerusalem's divorce and judgment. But Revelation 19 brings us to the wedding feast of the Bride and the Bridegroom.

Immediately after the destruction of Babylon (Jerusalem), Heaven announces the marriage of the Lamb (Rev. 19:6-10). The punishment of God's adulterous wife not only publicly established Christ's Kingdom (19:6), but it also gave a legal justification for Jesus' marriage to the Bride. From A.D. 30–A.D. 70, two redemptive systems existed on the earth at the same time: Christ's Kingdom and the old sacrificial system. After Jesus, the Old Covenant was "fading way" and obsolete. But it still existed.

The destruction of Jerusalem formally wiped away the old and made way for the new. God had legally nullified His covenant with Israel through divorce. Now He could legally take the Church as His bride.

Revelation tells us that the Bride made herself ready by maintaining her purity during these turbulent times. Throughout the New Testament and Revelation, Jesus exhorts believers to stay true under the pressure of persecution. Those that had were publicly married to the Lamb.

There is also a correlation between the wedding feast of Revelation 19 and the celebratory feast in Matthew 8. In Matthew, the centurion (a gentile) came to Jesus to heal his son. Jesus offered to travel to this man's house, but the centurion stated that there was no need. He believed that Jesus could heal his son from a distance. Jesus marveled at his faith and stated:

> "Assuredly, I say to you, I have not found such great faith, not even in Israel! And I say to you that many will come from east and west [outside of Israel, i.e. Gentiles], and sit down with Abraham, Isaac, and Jacob in the kingdom of heaven [thereby joining the house of God]. But the sons of the kingdom [the Jews] will be cast out into outer darkness. There will be weeping and gnashing of teeth."[214]

Revelation 18-21 records these events. The sons of the kingdom (the former kingdom, i.e. Israel) were cast out (Jerusalem was cut off from God). And the gentiles became God's new faithful Bride.

Many of the early church fathers understood that the destruction of Jerusalem vindicated Christianity against Judaism. Tertullian, in his third book against Marcion, said this about the destruction of Jerusalem:

---

214. Matthew 8:10-12

> "So likewise that conditional threat of the sword, "If ye
> refuse and hear me not, the sword shall devour you," has
> proved that it was Christ, for rebellion against whom
> they have perished."[215]

Hyppolytus also vindicated the church through Jerusalem's death: "Thou [Jerusalem] art dead in the world, but thou livest in Christ." [216]

Melito of Sardis often taught on Israel's arrogance against Jesus many times. In one of his sermons, he ends with Jesus' vindication through Jerusalem's destruction: "Therefore, O Israel, you did not quake in the presence of the Lord, so you quaked at the assault of foes... And you [Jerusalem] lie dead, but He has risen from the dead and gone up to the heights of heaven." [217]

The early church understood that the destruction of Jerusalem did two things: It proved that Jesus was the Messiah, and it vindicated the Church against Judaism as the true people of God.

The New Testament displays the full course of God's redemptive plan. The gradual revelation of the Kingdom

---

215. Tertullian, *Against Marcion*, 3.23.

216. Hippolytus of Rome, "Treatise on Christ and Antichrist," in *Fathers of the Third Century: Hippolytus, Cyprian, Novatian, Appendix*, ed. Alexander Roberts, James Donaldson, and A. Cleveland Coxe, trans. S. D. F. Salmond, vol. 5, The Ante-Nicene Fathers (Buffalo, NY: Christian Literature Company, 1886), 210.

217. Melito of Sardis, *On Pascha*, trans. S. G. Hall (Oxford: Clarendon Press, 1979), 55, 57.

through Jesus' ministry. Its legal establishment through Jesus' crucifixion and resurrection. And its public vindication with the destruction of Jerusalem.

The Church's Destiny Required Jerusalem's Destruction

Furthermore, the early church needed to be separated from Jerusalem in order to step into it's own destiny. When God destroyed the sacrificial system, it did two things. It put an end to many "Jewish" Christian ideas against which the early apostles argued (see Paul's discussion in Galatians). And it reoriented the early church away from Jerusalem and the Temple.

Early Christianity looked a lot like Judaism. Those outside of the Judeo-Christian world couldn't differentiate between Jews and Christians. They saw Christians as a type of Jew (and so did much of the early church).

Acts 1:6 reveals just how Jerusalem-focused the apostles were. When Jesus commissioned them, they asked if it was time for Jesus to "restore the kingdom to Israel." This reveals their deep belief that Jerusalem was at the center of God's redemptive plan. God had to break this mindset so they would spread the gospel throughout the world. After A.D. 70, it became obvious Jerusalem was no longer the center of His plan.

They also needed to realize that the Temple no longer played a role in their faith. Since the coming of the Spirit, there was no need for a Temple. Believers became the temple of God's presence. But the Temple was at the center of the Jewish faith, and this influenced how early Christians saw the world. The destruction of the Temple forced early Christians out of this mindset. The Temple was irrelevant and no longer needed. So God did away with it.

Jesus told the disciples that once the Holy Spirit came, they would be His witnesses in Judea and to the ends of the earth. Except for Paul, it took years and an act of God to get the disciples out of Jerusalem. They were so focused on Jerusalem that they didn't quite grasp the "ends of the earth" aspect of their mission.

The destruction of Jerusalem established Christianity as a separate religion from Judaism. It also refocused Christians away from Jerusalem and onto "making disciples of all nations." The period between A.D. 30 and A.D. 70 was very painful for the Church and the Jews ("birth pangs" Matt. 24:8), but it was also very important. The Church needed this dramatic reorientation to help her realize her ultimate mission and call.

The Death of the Beast – REVELATION 19:17-21

Revelation is more concerned with the judgment of Jerusalem, not the Beast. Therefore, the Beast's death is almost written as an afterthought. Revelation 19:19 states that the Beast makes war against the saints, but Christ slays the Beast.

Over the course of the next 300 years, Rome initiated several persecutions against the Church. But the Church continued to grow. Ultimately the Church consumed the Empire and destroyed her demonic authority. In this manner, Christ destroyed the Beast.

The Millennium
REVELATION 20

Interpreting the millennium has inspired passionate debate. But in any discussion about the millennium, we must remember that only ten verses in the most symbolic book of the Bible mention it.

Many believe that Christ will return around the rapture and the Great Tribulation. Then He will reign for a literal one thousand years. After which He will establish eternity.

Preterism believes that the millennium is symbolic. It represents a period of time that began in the first century and continues through today.

There is no reason to take the number one thousand literal. Most of the numbers in Revelation have been symbolic. Why would we start taking numbers literal now? The number ten often represents quantitative fulfillment in scripture (see Psalm 50:10).[218] One thousand is ten to the third power (three is also a big symbolic number, alerting the reader to special meaning).

Therefore, one thousand symbolizes the complete fulfillment of something. It represents the sum total of an

---

218. Kenneth Gentry Jr. and others, *Three Views on the Millennium and Beyond* (Grand Rapids, MI: Zondervan, 1999), 52.

object or span of time. We see one thousand used else-where in the Bible in this manner. For instance, Psalm 50:10 says that God owns a cattle on a thousand hills. We are not saying that God only owns cattle on a thousand hills. The author employed one thousand to communicate that God owns everything.

We can apply the same principle to the millennium. It isn't a literal one thousand years. It is however long it takes to complete the purpose of the millennium.

So, what is the purpose of the millennium? The grad-ual expansion of the Kingdom of God throughout the whole world.

We often see God's promises progressively fulfilled. Look at the Garden of Eden as an example. God told Adam and Eve to take dominion of the planet.[219] This implies that the area beyond the Garden was not yet cultivated. It was wild. The planet was theirs by promise, but they didn't yet physically possess it. It became theirs progressively.

Another example of this is the Promised Land. God told Joshua, "from the wilderness and this Lebanon as far as the great river, the River Euphrates, all the land of the Hittites, and to the Great Sea… shall be yours."[220] In promise, the land belonged to the Israelites. Yet, God also said, "And the LORD your God will drive out those

---

219. Genesis 1:28

220. Joshua 1:3-5

nations before you little by little; you will be unable to destroy them at once, lest the beasts of the field become too numerous for you."[221] Though the entire Promised Land belonged to the Jews at once, they took possession of it over time. The millennium is similar. The entire planet is ours, but we have to spread the Kingdom to make it a reality.

The Binding of Satan

For some, this interpretation of the millennium is problematic because Satan is supposed to be bound during the millennium (Rev. 20:3). And since evil still persists on the planet (i.e., Satan appears to be anything but bound), we can't be in the millennium.

But Revelation 20:3 doesn't say that Satan can't influence world events. It says that he can no longer deceive the nations:

> "He [Christ] laid hold of the dragon, that serpent of old, who is the Devil and Satan, and bound him for a thousand years… so that he should deceive the nations no more." (Rev. 20:2-3)

Before Christ, only the Jews had access to God. Satan had deceived the rest of the world into worshipping false gods. But when Jesus came, He destroyed Satan's kingdom. Then He opened the gospel to all peoples. Thus,

---

221. Deuteronomy 7:22

Christ bound Satan's ability to keep the nations deceived.

In this manner, Jesus judicially bound Satan two thousand years ago. And it is the church's job to enforce that binding around the world.

Furthermore, when God gave the Promised Land to the Israelites, He told them that "no man" would be able to stop them. Yet, Israelites met stiff resistance. They had to fight thousands of men to take the land. But the Canaanites could not stop them from inheriting their promise. This is like the millennium.

Christ defeated Satan (Matt. 28:18; Col. 2:15). Satan can resist us, but he cannot stop us. The millennium is the era of the Church. It will end when the Church fully retakes the planet from darkness.

The Reign of Christ

Christ's reign is also integrally linked to the millennium, and Christ reigns today. Christ established His kingdom in the first century (Matt. 28:18; Mark 1:14-15; Col. 2:15). Jesus declared that the Kingdom had come while He preached. He claimed to be king while on earth (John 18:36). And after His resurrection, He ascended to Heaven to sit at the right hand of the Father, where He currently reigns:

> "... which He worked in Christ when He raised Him from the dead and seated Him at His right hand in the heavenly places, far above all principality and power and might

and dominion, and every name that is named, not only in this age but also in that which is to come."[222]

"To him who overcomes I will grant to sit with Me on My throne, as I also overcame and sat down with My Father on His throne."[223]

"All authority on Heaven and on Earth has been given to Me..."[224]

Furthermore, scripture states that we are seated with Him and reign with Him now. It is not delayed until the future:

"[the Father] raised us up together, and made us sit together in the heavenly places in Christ Jesus"[225]

"If then you were raised with Christ, seek those things which are above, where Christ is, sitting at the right hand of God."[226]

"But you are a chosen generation, a royal priesthood, a holy nation, His own special people."[227]

---

222. Ephesians 1:20-21

223. Revelation 3:21

224. Matthew 28:18

225. Ephesians 2:6

226. Colossians 3:1

227. 1 Peter 2:9

And, finally, Jesus Himself:

> "All authority has been given to Me in heaven and on earth. Go therefore and make disciples of all the nations, baptizing them in the name of the Father and of the Son and of the Holy Spirit"[228]

John tells us that as He is in heaven (reigning over all of the Earth) so are we *in this world* (1 John 4:17). Jesus is King of the Earth. He rules through us as we advance His Kingdom. This is the millennium.

The Second Coming

Revelation is not about the end of the world or Christ's second coming. It is about the transfer of covenants between Israel and the Church. Thus, John only briefly mentions Jesus' second coming in Revelation 20:7-15. We can assume that this happens when the church finishes her mission. Then Satan will be thrown into the lake of fire. The living and the dead will be judged. And death itself will be destroyed.

The Reign of Death

Paul gives us further insight into Christ's second coming in I Corinthians. Some Corinthians were worried that they had missed Jesus' return. In this passage, Paul discusses the resurrection and its relationship to the return of Jesus:

---

228. Matthew 28:18-19

> "For as in Adam all die, so also in Christ shall all be made alive. But each in his own order: Christ the firstfruits, then at his coming those who belong to Christ. Then comes the end, when he delivers the kingdom to God the Father after destroying every rule and every authority and power. **For he must reign until he has put all his enemies under his feet. The last enemy to be destroyed is death.**"[229]

Paul states we shouldn't expect Jesus' return until after He has put all enemies under his feet. How is Jesus putting those principalities under His feet? Through the Church. We are to heal the sick, cleanse the leper, raise the dead, and cast out demons. We're called to destroy the works of the devil. We're told to do this until He returns. He will return when it is done. It will be done when every principality falls to His name. And the final principality to fall will be death itself.

This has startling implications for Jesus' return. We are supposed to spread the Kingdom of God until people stop dying. Only then can we expect Jesus' return.

This changes the way we see our purpose on the planet. Jesus came to save the world, not destroy it. He took dominion of the planet in the first century. He has commissioned us to fight His war to restore the Kingdom of God. We are not to predict the end of the world. We are supposed to bring the world into its purpose. We are here to redeem the planet. We are here to co-labor with Christ to make a New Heaven and a New Earth.

---

229. 1 Corinthians 15:22-26 ESV, emphasis added.

Chapter 7

A NEW HEAVEN AND A NEW EARTH

The last 2 chapters of Revelation reveal the times in which we live. They discuss the Bride and the New Jerusalem. This section of Revelation can be confusing because of how it talks about the Bride and the New Jerusalem. Many think that it is discussing two different entities. But they are one and the same:

> "Then one of the seven angels... came and talked with me, saying, 'Come, I will show you the bride, the Lamb's wife.' And he carried me away in the Spirit to a great and high mountain, and showed me the great city, the holy Jerusalem, descending out of heaven from God."[230]

The angel takes John to see the Bride. But John sees the New Jerusalem instead. We are forced to conclude that they are the same, and represent the Church.

---

230. Revelation 21:9–10.

These last two chapters of Revelation are about the Church's purpose in the world. We are here to reveal the New Heaven and the New Earth:

> "Now I saw a new heaven and a new earth, for the first heaven and the first earth had passed away. Also there was no more sea. Then I, John, saw the holy city, New Jerusalem, coming down out of heaven from God, prepared as a bride adorned for her husband."[231]

Revelation 21:1 appears to be a fulfillment of Isaiah 65:17-25:

> "For behold, I create new heavens and a new earth;
> And the former shall not be remembered or come
>   to mind…
> Never again will there be in it
> Infants who live but a few days,
> Or older people who do not live out their years;
> Those who die at a hundred
> Will be thought mere youths;
> Those who fail to reach a hundred
> Will be considered accursed….
> The wolf and the lamb will feed together,
> And the lion will eat straw like the ox,
> But dust will be the serpent's food.
> They will neither harm nor destroy
> On all my holy mountain." (Isaiah 65:17, 20, 25)

The correlation between these two passages is too similar to ignore. They both state that God has created a "new

---

231. Revelation 21:1-2

heaven and new earth." They both say that He has rebuilt Jerusalem into a beautiful new city. It appears that John intentionally depicted Revelation 21 as the fulfillment of Isaiah 65:17. Let's take a closer look at these similarities and their implications.

First, notice the similarity between the language in Isaiah 65:17 with Revelation 21:1:

> "**For behold, I create new heavens and a new earth**; and the former shall not be remembered or come to mind"[232]

> "**Now I saw a new heaven and a new earth**, for the first heaven and the first earth had passed away."[233]

These two passages appear to be discussing the same event. Isaiah predicted it and John saw it happen. This means we need to understand Revelation 21 as the fulfillment of Isaiah 65. Which anchors Revelation 21 before the consummation of eternity.

Isaiah 65 is often considered a prophetic statement about eternity. This passage depicts a utopian future free from the horrors of our current world.

But notice that in Isaiah 65:20 people are still dying. It claims that "those who die at a hundred will be thought mere youths; those who fail to reach a hundred will be considered accursed." Unless we want to claim that aging

---

232. Isaiah 65:17, emphasis added.

233. Revelation 21:1, emphasis added.

and death still exist in eternity, we must anchor Isaiah 65:17-25 on this side of heaven.

Since Revelation 21:1 identifies itself as the fulfillment of Isaiah 65:17-25, Revelation 21:1 is also a now verse.

Furthermore, in Revelation, these events occurred right after the fall of Jerusalem. This means that we are living in this period.

We haven't seen the complete fulfillment of these promises, but it reveals our duty as the Church. We are to make these promises a reality in the world.

For some, this may seem to contradict the sovereignty of God. It appears to place too much authority in the Church, and leaves God subject to our actions. But we have distorted the meaning of "sovereignty."

Today, the sovereignty of God means that everything that happens is part of God's plan. But sovereignty means that God answers to no higher power.

When we say that a country is "sovereign" we are not saying the government controls every action within its borders. We mean that it answers to no other nation.

In the same way, God answers to no other power. But He is not in control of everything. He could not be in control and give us free will at the same time.

Furthermore, Jesus taught us to pray, "Your kingdom come, Your will be done on Earth as it is in Heaven" (Matt. 6:9-10). If His will were already being done, why would He have us pray for it?

Since the Church co-labors with Christ, we are partially responsible for bringing the Kingdom to earth. This means that the promises within Isaiah 65 are available to us. It is our mission to bring them into reality.

It also places a lot of authority on the shoulders of the Church. As we expand the Kingdom throughout the world, we will see a decline in evil and these promises fulfilled.

Revelation 21-22 illustrates the progressive advancement of the Kingdom across the earth.

Revelation 21-22 also describes the wedding of the Bride of Christ. We were married to Him two thousand years ago. Throughout the New Testament, Scripture refers to the Church as the Bride of Christ (see Eph. 5:25-33; 2 Cor. 11:2-3).

There is no perceived gap between the destruction of Jerusalem and the wedding feast. In fact, the destruction of Jerusalem makes the wedding feast legal. After her divorce, the immediate appearance of the New Jerusalem makes logical sense. Otherwise God would have divorced one people and waited thousands of years to marry a new people. But, in the Old Testament, God was Israel's "husband" because of their covenant. This implies that we are now God's husband because of our covenant with Him.

Finally, Revelation clearly states that these events must occur soon after John recorded them:

> "The Lord God of the holy prophets sent His angel to show His servants the things **which must shortly take place**."[234]

---

234. Revelation 22:6, emphasis added.

"Behold, I [Jesus] am **coming quickly!**"[235]

"'Do not seal the words of the prophecy of this book, for **the time is at hand**.'"[236]

"And behold, I am **coming quickly.**"[237]

"He who testifies to these things says, 'Surely I am **coming quickly**.'"[238]

Jesus states *three* times within the last 20 verses of Revelation that He is "coming quickly." Jesus and an angel tell John *five separate* times that these events would take place *very soon*. They did not mean "more than two thousand years later." Jesus said that His words were "faithful and true," and He said that the events recorded in Revelation would occur within John's lifetime. And because of everything we've already discussed, it is clear that He did come, and that He now reigns while His Kingdom expands throughout the earth.

The Signs of the Times

Let's look at a few verses from the final two chapters of

---

235. Revelation 22:7, emphasis added.

236. Revelation 22:10, emphasis added.

237. Revelation 22:12, emphasis added.

238. Revelation 22:20, emphasis added.

Revelation to see how they describe our present reality.

Revelation 21:3 -

"Behold, the tabernacle of God is with men, and He will
dwell with them, and they shall be His people. God Himself will be with them and be their God."

Do we not live in this time? Does God not dwell in our
hearts? Jesus said that He would tear down the Temple
and rebuild it in three days (John 2:19). He did this
when He tore down the old covenant, and established
the Church. The presence of God used to dwell in the
Temple. Now His presence lives in our hearts. We have
unmitigated access to the Father through the indwell-
ing of the Holy Spirit. Furthermore, Paul states that our
bodies are now "the temple of the Holy Spirit" (I Cor.
6:19), implying that Revelation 21:3 began two thousand
years ago.

Revelation 21:4a–

"And God will wipe away every tear from their eyes…"

This describes our salvation and the outpouring of the
Holy Spirit. Much of the Church is trapped in a desert
existence. They live with wounds in their hearts waiting
to enter into the Promised Land (i.e., go to Heaven). They
don't realize that God brought the Promised Land to us

through the Holy Spirit. As we walk in the presence of the Spirit, God heals every wound and wipes away every tear. The fact that so many Christians are living outside of this reality reveals how far the devil has deceived the Bride. It is tragic that so many Christians are not experiencing all that God has for them.

Revelation 21:4b–

"There shall be no more death, nor sorrow, nor crying."

Jesus said that all who believe in Him would not die. They would receive eternal life (John. 3:16; 11:25). He states: "He who believes in Me, though he may die, he shall live." Our souls have been snatched from hell and are secured in Christ for eternity. Even though our bodies die, we don't. Why can't John be saying the same thing in Revelation? He did write both books.

Furthermore, as we have already discussed, death will be the final enemy of the Church to fall. So there will come a day when people stop dying, and this verse will become a reality on the earth.

Revelation 21:4c–

"There shall be no more pain, for the former things have passed away."

Paul describes our conversion experience the same way. He said that the "old things have passed away" and that "all things are made new" (2 Cor. 5:17). We are a new creation. We are to "forget" those things that lie behind and press on to the things ahead (Phil. 3:13-14).

As the knowledge of the glory of the Lord covers the earth, we will no longer remember the former things. This is already being fulfilled. How many people in the modern world "remember" what it was like to starve? Or die of plague? Or live under tyranny? Or constantly fear that an invading army would kill your husband, rape your wife, and enslave your children? We have a long way to go, but we have also come far.

Revelation, Daniel, and Isaiah all tell us that we are in this period of time. The kingdom is advancing. It will continue to advance until the knowledge of the glory of the Lord covers the earth as the waters cover the seas (Habakkuk 2:14).

Revelation 22:1–

> "And he showed me a pure river of water of life, clear as crystal, proceeding from the throne of God and of the Lamb."

Jesus says that all who come to Him will have a river of life gushing from their chests (John 7:37-38). This water comes from the throne of God in our hearts. This is not something reserved for eternity. It is for today.

Revelation 22:2a –

> "In the middle of its street, and on either side of the river, was the tree of life, which bore twelve fruits, each tree yielding its fruit every month."

Each tree bore fruit all year long, meaning God's kingdom will bear fruit in all seasons without end.

Revelation 22:2b –

> "The leaves of the tree were for the healing of the nations."

If Revelation 22 is about eternity, why would the nations need healing? Wouldn't they have already been healed? This verse illustrates the role of the Church within the world today. We are those leaves. We are here to heal the nations ("Make disciples of all nations..." Matt. 28:18).

In describing the destiny of the Church, Dr. Gentry summarizes Revelation 21 -22 well:

> "Revelation 21:1-8 informs us that this new creation salvation removes grief (Rev. 21:4;), introduces one into the family of God (Rev. 21:7;), and brings eternal life (Rev. 21:6). Revelation 21:9-22:5 speaks of the majesty of the bride-church. She shines brilliantly like light (21:10-11). She has a secure foundation and impregnable walls (Rev. 21:12-21). Thus, she is destined to have a massive influence in the world (Rev. 21:16). She is cared for by God's provision with the water of life (Rev. 21:22; 22:1-5). Thus, she brings healing to nations by her presence (Rev. 22:2-3)."[239]

---

239. Gentry and others, *Four Views on the Book of Revelation*, 90.

As we can see, the Church is destined to do great things. It is our mandate to redeem the earth.

Chapter 8

PROGRESSIVE REDEMPTION

"Therefore, if anyone is in Christ, he is a new creation; old things have passed away; behold, all
things have become new." – II Cor. 5:17

One of the greatest tragedies of the Western Church is
the belief that Revelation is about the end of the world.
This has left the Church virtually powerless in the world
today by putting it on the defensive. Instead of seeking
the planet's redemption, many are declaring its judgment.

Revelation is about God's divorce of Jerusalem and
His marriage to the Church. It is about the futility of the
old covenant, and the destiny of the new.

For many people, this paradigm shift is massive and
uncomfortable. It feels like heresy to say that Revelation
isn't about the end of the world. This reorientation can
be very unsettling. Many people have built their faith
on a futurist understanding of the world. Even though

preterism maintains the divinity of Christ, it can feel like your faith has been challenged. But wrestling with these ideas is important. It will refine you, even if you choose to maintain a futurist interpretation of scripture.

Revelation has the ability to change your life and empower you to step into your destiny. It can bolster the church as she advances the Kingdom around the world.

This deception about Revelation has beguiled us into giving Satan the planet. If he can convince us that everything is going to get worse, then we won't try to stop it. We have given Satan free reign to do evil. We are expecting it. In a way, we are empowering it through our faith that it will happen. Some well-intentioned Christians even pray for these things in order to hasten the second coming of Christ. Satan has convinced some to pray for his will, not the Father's.

When we pray for Jesus to return, we are condemning over half of the planet to destruction. It is a death sentence to four billion people. But Jesus said He didn't come to destroy men's lives, but to save them (Luke 9:54).

Many Christians also believe that working to better the planet violates God's will. It if tis God's will to destroy the planet, then striving to better it puts us in direct opposition to God's plan.

When confronted with a new interpretation, there are many reactions. Some people have wrapped their identity in futurism so tightly that they are forced to defend it. Some may even say that the "facts" can't be trusted. Even though statistics say the world is getting better, it must be a deception. Thus, we need to live by "faith alone."

But once we abandon reason, we destine ourselves to death. At some point we have to decide that we can trust our senses. We need to believe that we can know reality. Otherwise, how can we know anything at all? Up can be down. Right can be wrong. Once we have made the choice to ignore what we observe, anything is possible.

If the world isn't getting worse, and if the Bible doesn't support a futurist worldview, what does that mean for the Church today? It radically changes our purpose. We are Daniel's stone of Daniel 2. Instead of stewarding a diminishing church, we have inherited the Kingdom of Daniel 7. We are expected to expand it and to loot the kingdom of Satan just as Jesus commanded in Matthew 28.

Isaiah declares that, "Of the increase of His government and peace there will be no end" (Isaiah 9:7). That Kingdom was established two thousand years ago. We are the administrators of that Kingdom as it expands over the world. Instead of watching the planet crumble, we have been commissioned to redeem the fallen world into the likeness of Heaven (Matt. 6:10).

The Progressive Nature of the Kingdom

Many believe that once Heaven comes, it will be instantaneous. They reject the idea of a progressive fulfillment of the millennium. It doesn't match their understanding of eternity and seems to steal the hope we have in it. It appears to state that eternity will be just like today.

Once the Kingdom of God fully manifests, there will be no more evil. We still have that as our hope. But this will not happen overnight. We will push back evil until we extinguish it.

Jesus often described the Kingdom as something that starts small yet grows to be large. In other words, it is a process, not instantaneous. For instance, He said that the Kingdom was like a mustard seed.

> "A man took [a mustard seed] and sowed it in his field, which indeed is the least of all the seeds; but when it is grown it is greater than the herbs and becomes a tree, so that the birds of the air come and nest in its branches." (Matt. 13:31-32).

The Kingdom started small (twelve men), yet it has become the world's largest and fastest growing religion.

In another instance, Jesus compares the Kingdom to yeast in bread. It is small at first, but expands throughout the entire loaf, causing it to rise (Matt. 13:33). Again, this has happened today. Even though many do not recognize it, the Kingdom of God has begun to permeate even the secular world.

For example, modern forms of government are based upon Christian ethics. Are they perfect reflections of the Kingdom? No, but they are better than what was previously there. The environmental movement is another example. Though they are not part of the Church, men and women all over the world have realized that we need to steward the planet (Gen. 1:28). Is everything they stand for aligned with Christ? No, but it is an improvement from where we were. Everywhere you look the Father's heart is being reflected all over the planet to a greater degree.

Though Jesus said He had all authority (Matt. 28:18), we are still in conflict. Paul states that we war against "powers and principalities." And that Christ will not return until all principalities bow to His name. Daniel 7 says that the beasts had their power taken away, but they were allowed to remain for a while. Revelation states that Satan was bound in his ability to deceive the nations. But it does not say that he is unable to influence world events. We are here to progressively advance the Kingdom and push this evil out of the land.

Planetary Conversion

The world still experiences turmoil because it is still under a curse. It won't be released from that curse until we understand our identity in Christ. When Adam fell, so did creation:

> "Cursed is the ground for your sake; In toil you shall eat of it All the days of your life. Both thorns and thistles it shall bring forth for you."[240]

God said that the planet was cursed "for your sake," meaning Adam's fall. This means that the planet–the

---

240. Genesis 3:17-18

dirt, the trees, and the animals–is not operating as God planned. The earth's corruption is linked to our fall. Thus, it is also linked to our redemption.

Paul states the world is groaning for redemption:

> "For the earnest expectation of the creation eagerly waits for the **revealing of the sons of God.** For the creation was subjected to futility, not willingly, but because of Him who subjected it in hope; because the creation itself **also will be delivered from the bondage of corruption** into the glorious liberty of the children of God. For we know that **the whole creation groans and labors with birth pangs** together until now."[241]

Paul says the earth is "groaning" under the weight of "corruption." Earthquakes, tsunamis, hurricanes, tornados, and other natural disasters are not judgments from God. The earth is groaning for the sons of God to realize who they are. This is how the world will be released from its bondage. As more people step out of darkness, the earth will be released from the curse.

Baptized in Fire

This planetary conversion will resemble something like ours. People often use 2 Peter 3:10 to defend a fiery judgment of the planet. But it actually supports global redemption:

---

241. Romans 8:19-22, emphasis added.

> "But the day of the Lord will come as a thief in the night, in which the heavens will pass away with a great noise, and the elements will melt with fervent heat; both the earth and the works that are in it will be burned up."[242]

From this verse, many people think that fire will consume the world on the Last Day. So much so that the material elements (rock, trees, air, etc.) will melt in God's judgment. But the Greek reveals that this is not true.

The word used in 2 Peter 3:10 for "elements" is *stoicheion*. It translates as "elementary principles," not the material elements of the planet. The Analytical Lexicon of the Greek New Testament says this about *stoicheion*:

> "(1) Generally, the rudimentary elements of anything, what belongs to a basic series in any field of knowledge; in grammar, the ABCs; in speech, basic sounds... (2) As used in the NT; (a) as a religious technical term for elementary doctrines, fundamental teachings, basic principles... (b) in a negative sense, humanistic teachings common to Jewish and pagan religions, involving binding traditions, taboos, prohibitions, ordinances, ceremonies, etc..."

It goes on to say that it can mean the natural elements of the planet. But the only reference it uses for this interpretation is 2 Peter 3:10.

Scripture uses *stoicheion* three other times (Col. 2:8, Gal. 4:3, Heb. 5:12). In each case, our bibles translate it as the "elementary principles of the world." 2 Peter is the

---

242. 2 Peter 3:10

281

only place where we translate *stoicheion* it as the basic, material principles of the earth. This implies that our eschatology has influenced our translation of 2 Peter 3:10.

Moreover, the end of the verse supports a planetary conversion interpretation, not judgment. The New King James renders the end of the verse as: "the world and the works that are in it will be burned up." The NIV, ESV, and NLT all say that the world and all its works will be "exposed" or "laid bare" or "seen as deserving judgment."

There is a difference between being "burned up" and being "exposed." With one, fire consumes the world. With the other, people see the world for what it is: fallen. And this is exactly what we should expect as the gospel advances around the planet. People will recognize that the old way of life deserved judgment. But judgment is not imputed because of the cross.

When you were saved, you were baptized in water and fire (Luke 3:16). Paul tells us that the old things passed away and all things became new (2 Cor. 5:17). In the salvation process, the Holy Spirit must show you why you need salvation. So, He must reveal how you have been living your life and moves you to repentance. The former things are "exposed" and "laid bare." At this point, many fall down before God, aware that they deserve judgment.

But God didn't judge you. He saved and redeemed you. Why should we expect God to treat the planet any different?

Peter is saying that God will baptize the planet in fire just like He baptized you. The former ways of thinking and living will be "exposed" and "seen as deserving judgment." Humanity will reject them and the earth will be freed from her bondage.

When you were born again you still looked the same. But Paul states that you are now a new creation (2 Cor. 5:17). And though you are new, you are awaiting final consummation. The same is true for the planet.

What will this gradual conversion experience look like? Revelation 21-22 and Isaiah 65 tell us. Past sorrows and pains will fade away (Is. 65:17; Rev. 21:4). Joy will grow throughout the Church and the world (Is. 65:18). The world will delight in the church because of the blessing it brings (Is. 65:18; Rev. 22:2). Weeping and crying will end (Is. 65:19; Rev. 21:4). Infant mortality rates and miscarriages will diminish (Is. 65:20). Life expectancies will grow (Is. 65:20). Death itself will waste away (Is. 65:20; Rev. 21:4). Predators will become herbivores and befriend their former prey (Is. 65:25). Evil governments will give way to righteous ones (Rev. 22:2). Freedom will advance across the earth (Rev. 22:2).

Also examine Isaiah 60:

"Arise, and shine; For your light has come! And the glory of the Lord is risen upon you. For behold, the darkness shall cover the earth, And deep darkness the people; But the Lord will arise over you, And His glory will be seen upon you. The Gentiles shall come to your light, And kings to the brightness of your rising.

"Then you shall see and become radiant, And your heart shall swell with joy; Because the abundance of the sea shall be turned to you, The wealth of the Gentiles shall come to you."[243]

This passage states that darkness will cover the earth and a deep darkness the people. Darkness does not cover the earth in eternity. This verse is meant for today. Yet the emphasis is not placed upon the darkness, but rather the redemptive effect we have on the planet. Revelation 21:22-25 says this time has come:

"The city [The New Jerusalem, the Bride of Christ] had no need of the sun or of the moon to shine in it, **for the glory of God illuminated it**. The Lamb is its light. And the nations of those who are saved shall **walk in its light**, and the **kings of the earth bring their glory and honor into it**. Its gates shall not be shut at all by day (**there shall be no night there**)."

Isaiah said that we were to "arise and shine, for our light has come." John states that God will illuminate the New Jerusalem. Isaiah says that the gentiles will come to our light. John states that the kings of the earth will be attracted to our light. Isaiah says the abundance of the gentiles will come to us. John says the rulers of the earth will honor and glorify the New Jerusalem, the Church.

Satan has convinced us that we have no authority here and that we should just wait for Jesus to return. But it is our call and mission to retake the planet. It is our joy to bring the fulfillment of these promises to the earth.

---

243. Isaiah 60:1-3, 5, emphasis added.

Chapter 9

CONCLUDING THOUGHTS

"In Your presence is fullness of joy;
At   Your   right   hand   are   pleasures
    forevermore." – Psalm 16:11

With such a dramatic departure from our understandings of scripture, many may be left wondering what to do next. This view of the end times can unsettle our understanding of what it means to be a Christian.

But it is exciting, because it means that God has placed us here for a purpose far beyond saving souls. He wants souls saved, but that is not the end goal of His plan. He wants a redeemed planet, with sons and daughters who understand their royal identity as children of the King and co-heirs with Christ. He places certain passions and gifts within our hearts to do His will on the earth. Part of our job as Christians is to discover what these are. Then we get to live out the adventure.

God likes art, fashion, music, and entertainment. He wants a godly government, Kingdom movies, and restored neighborhoods. And He wants us to do it.

We were put here with a purpose. He prepared good works for us (ones that fulfill the desires of our hearts) before the beginning of time (Eph. 2:10). His will on earth originates as a desire inside our hearts.

So, search your heart. Dare to dream those dreams you haven't dreamt since you were a kid. In them you may find your purpose and your calling. You were not placed here to announce the end, but to usher in the beginning. You were not put here to labor in vein, but to transform the planet through the passions of your heart.

God's original plan for us was to live life on earth. He wants us to live with overflowing joy on a redeemed planet. It is our mission to make that a reality. When we are done, He will return and raise those from the dead who came before us. Then we will all live in eternity on the planet that we helped rebuild. This is how we are co-laborers with Christ. Now is the time for the Church to rise and change history. We can do it. It is our destiny.

What Now?

This book was not meant to discuss what the church should be doing today in detail. It was about eschatology. How we live out our faith as the Body of Christ is the subject of many other books. To learn more about your specific destiny and purpose, you should read the books listed below. Thank you for taking the time to read *The End of Days: The Shocking Truth About The Times In Which We Live.*

For Further Reading

- *When Heaven Invades Earth*, by Bill Johnson

- *How Heaven Invades Earth* (formerly know as *Heavy Rain*), by Kris Vallotton

- *Secrets to Imitating God* [formerly known as *Dreaming with God*], by Bill Johnson

- *The Supernatural Ways of Royalty*, by Kris Vallotton and Bill Johnson

- *Developing A Supernatural Lifestyle*, by Kris Vallotton

Further Reading on Eschatology

- *Four Views on the Book of Revelation*

- *Three Views on the Millennium*

- *Victorious Eschatology*

BIBLIOGRAPHY

Al Katani, Ahmed. Web-Archive of Al-Jazeera Interview, "Interview with Sheikh Ahmed Al Katani on the Christianization of Africa," December 12, 2012: http://web. archive.org/web/20040402023134/www.aljazeera.net/ programs/shareea/articles/2000/12/12-6.htm, accessed on May 11, 2012.

Bass, Clarence B. *Backgrounds to Dispensationalism*. Eugene, OR: Wipf and Stock Publishers, 2005.

Boatwright, Mary T., Daniel J. Gargola, and Richard J. A. Talbert. *The Romans: From Village to Empire*. New York, NY: Oxford University Press, 2004.

Bock, Darrell L., Craig A. Blaising, Kenneth L. Gentry Jr., and Robert B. Strimple. *Three Views on the Millennium and Beyond.* Grand Rapids, MI: Zondervan, 1999.

Brown, Francis, Samuel Rolles Driver, and Charles Augustus Briggs. *Enhanced Brown-Driver-Briggs Hebrew and English Lexicon*. Oak Harbor, WA: Logos Research Systems, 2000.

The Center for Disease Control, National Center for Health Statistics. *Birth Rates for US Teenagers Reach Historic Lows for All Age and Ethnic Groups.* NCHS Data Brief, No. 89, April 2012.

Chrysostom, John Chrysostom. "Homilies of St. John
    Chrysostom, Archbishop of Constantinople on the Gospel
    According to St. Matthew," in *Saint Chrysostom: Hom-
    ilies on the Gospel of Saint Matthew*, ed. Philip Schaff,
    trans. George Prevost and M. B. Riddle, vol. 10, A Select
    Library of the *Nicene and Post-Nicene Fathers of the
    Christian Church*, First Series. New York: Christian Lit-
    erature Company, 1888.

Eberle, Harold and Martin Trench. *Victorious Eschatology:
    A Partial Preterist View, 2ⁿᵈ Edition.* Yakima, WA: World-
    cast Publishing, 2009.

Ellis, Edwards. *The Making of the New Testament Docu-
    ments*. Atlanta, GA: Society of Biblical Literature, 1999.

Epiphanius. *The Panarion of Epiphanius of Salamis: Book
    1*. Translated by Frank Williams. Koninklijke Brill NV,
    Leiden, The Netherlands: 2009.

Eusebius. *Church History, Life of Constantine the Great,
    and Oration in Praise of Constantine*. Edited by Philip
    Schaff and Henry Wace. Translated by Arthur Cushman
    McGiffert. *The Nicene and Post-Nicene Fathers of the
    Christian Church*, Second Series. New York: Christian
    Literature Company, 1890.

Eusebius. *The Proof of the Gospel*. Translated. by W.J.
    Ferrar. *Translations Of Christian Literature, Series I.* The
    Macmillan Company,   New York, Ny: 1920.

Bibliography

Friberg, Timothy, Barbara Friberg and Neva F. Miller. Volume 4. *Analytical Lexicon of the Greek New Testament*. Baker's Greek New Testament library. Grand Rapids, Mich.: Baker Books, 2000.

Fee, Gordon. *Paul, the Spirit, and the People of God*. Peabody, MA: 1996.

Food and Agriculture Organization. "Hunger Report." Accessed on July 28th, 2011: http://hungerreport.org/2011/data/hunger

Goklany, Indur. *The Improving State of the World: Why We're Living Longer, Healthier, More Comfortable Lives On A Cleaner Planet*. Washington, D.C.: Cato Institute, 2007.

Hippolytus of Rome, "Treatise on Christ and Antichrist," in *Fathers of the Third Century: Hippolytus, Cyprian, Novatian, Appendix*. Edited by Alexander Roberts, James Donaldson, and A. Cleveland Coxe. Translated by S. D. F. Salmond. Volume 5, *The Ante-Nicene Fathers*. Buffalo, NY: Christian Literature Company, 1886.

Irenaeus of Lyons, "Irenæus Against Heresies," in *The Apostolic Fathers with Justin Martyr and Irenaeus*, 5.30.3. Edited by Alexander Roberts, James Donaldson, and A. Cleveland Coxe. *Volume 1, The Ante-Nicene Fathers*. Buffalo, NY: Christian Literature Company, 1885.

Josephus, Flavius. *The Works of Josephus: Complete and*

Unabridged. Translated by William Whiston. Peabody, MA: Hendrickson Publishers, Inc., 1987.

Lisa Ling, "Our America with Lisa Ling: Faith Healers," Season 1, Episode 1. Los Angeles, CA: Oprah Winfrey Network: OWN, February 2011.

Pate, Marvin, Kenneth Gentry Jr., Sam Hamstra Jr., and Robert Homas. *Four Views on the Book of Revelation.* Grand Rapids, MI: Zondervan, 1998.

Pomeroy, Sarah B., Stanley M. Burstein, Walter Donlan, Jennifer Tolbert Roberts. *Ancient Greece: A Political, Social, and Cultural History, 2nd Edition.* New York, NY: Oxford University Press, 2008.

Martin, Michael. *The New American Commentary ,Volume 33.* Nashville: Broadman & Holman Publishers, 1995.

Martyr, Justin. "The First Apology of Justin,." *The Ante-Nicene Fathers, Vol 1,* Buffalo, NY: Christian Literature Company, 1885.

McKenzie, Steven. *How to Read the Bible : History, Prophecy, Literature.* New York, NY: Oxford University Press, 2005.

Melito of Sardis. *On Pascha and other Fragments.* Translated by S. G. Hall. Oxford: Clarendon Press, 1979.

Bibliography

Mounce, Robert. *The Book of Revelation.* Eerdmand Publishing Company, Grand Rapids, MI: 1998.

Scofield, C. I.. *Scofield Reference Bible.* New York, NY: Oxford University Press, 1917.

Scofield, C. I.. *Rightly Dividing the Word of God.* Oakland, CA: Western Book and Tract Co..

Swanson, James. *Dictionary of Biblical Languages With Semantic Domains: Hebrew (Old Testament)*, electronic ed., DBLH 3707. Oak Harbor: Logos Research Systems, Inc., 1997.

Tacitus. *Histories.* Translated by the Church and Brodribb. Macmillan, London: 1877.

Tertullian. "The Five Books Against Marcion," in *Latin Christianity: Its Founder, Tertullian.* Edited by Alexander Roberts, James Donaldson, and A. Cleveland Coxe. Translated Peter Holmes. Volume 3, *The Ante-Nicene Fathers.* Buffalo, NY: Christian Literature Company, 1885.

Trotter, William. *Plain Papers on Prophetic Subjects.* New York, NY: Loizeaux Brothers, New Edition, Revised.

Wright, N.T.. *The New Testament and the Kingdom of God.* Minneapolis, MN: Fortress Press, 1992.

www.ingramcontent.com/pod-product-compliance
Lightning Source LLC
Chambersburg PA
CBHW051820040426
42447CB00006B/289